Gain Social Awareness and Become Socially Perceptive!

How to Read Social Cues, Emotions, Behavior, and Intentions

By Patrick King

Social Interaction and Conversation Coach at
www.PatrickKingConsulting.com

Table of Contents

INTRODUCTION — 5

CHAPTER 1: LEARNING TO LISTEN—TO EVERYTHING — 11

PEOPLE WATCHING	12
THE FOUR CS OF BODY LANGUAGE	20
HOW TO READ THE VOICE	28
INTERPRETING SMILES	36

CHAPTER 2: HOW TO READ THE ROOM — 47

KNOWING WHEN THE CONVERSATION IS OVER	48
COOPERATIVE OVERLAPPING	56
SIX CLUES TO CHARACTER	65
THE SERVER TEST	74

CHAPTER 3: CHALLENGE YOUR ASSUMPTIONS TO BUILD REAL EMPATHY — 81

THE ILLUSION OF ASYMMETRIC INSIGHT	82
SUSAN FISKE'S STEREOTYPE CONTENT MODEL	90
BECOMING A TUNING FORK	100
DEVELOPING EMPATHY TO READ PEOPLE	108

CHAPTER 4: UNDERSTAND PEOPLE BY UNDERSTANDING THE LANGUAGE THEY USE — 121

THE "FOUR EARS" MODEL	122
DETECTING WEASEL WORDS	130

ONE BIG QUESTION	**138**
IDENTIFYING PEOPLE'S VALUES	**146**

CHAPTER 5: DIGGING DEEPER TO LEARN WHAT REALLY MAKES PEOPLE TICK   157

THE THREE LEVELS OF KNOWING A PERSON	**158**
MELTDOWNS, TANTRUMS, AND CORE FEARS	**165**
WHAT PEOPLE'S FRIENDSHIPS SAY ABOUT THEM	**173**
PREDICTING SOCIAL BEHAVIOR	**181**

Introduction

We live in a world where most people are desperate to be understood. We value self-knowledge and self-expression, we prize self-awareness and authenticity, and we hope that if we continue to look within for long enough, we will discover the secrets within our own deepest psychological depths.

In the process of all the contemplation, however, we can lose sight of something else important: other people.

While many today struggle valiantly to expand their own self-knowledge, the rarer and more underappreciated skill is actually the ability to understand other people. In other words, how many of us have the goal to understand first, rather than to be understood?

If you've picked up this book, chances are that on some level you're ready to upgrade your own ability to engage with, understand, and "read" people. The irony is that turning your focused attention *outside* of yourself may ultimately be the best way to develop self-knowledge.

We'll begin with a straightforward question: How good a judge of character are you?

In this book, you'll learn how to analyze people, how to understand complex social dynamics, and how to speak and listen to what people are *really* communicating about themselves. We don't do all of this in some passive, unengaged way, however. Rather, becoming people-readers improves our own lives in many different ways. Better people-reading skills allow us to:

- Know exactly who we're dealing with at all times. This gives us clarity and insight into the people around us and empowers us to make good choices for ourselves, whether that's in our personal or professional lives.
- Overcome social anxiety, awkwardness, and shyness
- Be more conscious and intentional in our social lives
- Make friends more easily and have more harmonious romantic relationships

- Get along better with clients, colleagues, and superiors
- Understand exactly how to be more persuasive and to get our point across clearly so others can hear it
- Detect deception and avoid being taken advantage of
- Reduce confusion and misunderstandings in social situations
- Develop our own charm, charisma, trustworthiness, and likeability
- Avoid conflict and become an overall better communicator and be perceived as more empathetic
- Finally, know ourselves better and gain a richer understanding of who we are relative to others around us

This book is not merely about becoming better at reading body language or learning to make quick but accurate judgments about people's personalities (although it will teach you that!). Rather, it will encourage you to become a more fully rounded, creative, and imaginative social being who can engage to the fullest with your social environment and all the fascinating and complicated people you find inhabiting it.

The more you challenge your own assumptions and biases, the more you get out of your bubble . . . and into other people's bubbles. With consistent daily practice, you learn to sharpen your skills of observation and inference so that soon the social world transforms before your eyes and suddenly becomes more intricate, enjoyable, and rewarding than you ever thought possible.

In the chapters that follow, we'll be opening up the social world and taking a peek at the hidden mechanisms lying under the hood. We'll begin with simple observation and the art of learning to listen above all else—that means listening to the body, too. We'll consider the fundamental rules of people watching that underpin everything, and armed with these skills, you'll be better able to "read the room."

You'll learn how to recognize when people are losing interest and want the conversation to end, how to interpret interruptions, and how to read tiny clues to people's characters, despite the masks they may wear. By countering the natural human instinct for distorted interpretations of others, you will gradually learn to let go of your own prejudices and witness people as they really are. It's only then that you are able to cultivate genuine empathy.

We'll explore ways to listen to what people say, the language they use, the things they don't say, their expressions, their reactions to others—in other words every part of an ocean of information that has always been there, just waiting to be explored. With practice, the skills and techniques described in these pages can help you become not just a more sophisticated people-reader, but a sound judge of character and a person able to truly comprehend others in terms of their own values, core fears, and predictable behaviors.

A warning, however: Our project is not a passive one! **Reading about people is not the same as people-reading**, and so the only way to make the principles discussed here come alive is to practically apply them. That's why throughout this book you'll be advised to take practical steps in your own social reality, try out some of the techniques, or just pay more attention to what you might not have noticed before. It's from these direct experiences that you'll learn the most.

Keep an open mind, commit yourself to putting in a little effort, and be willing to be surprised—one of the greatest rewards of being a dedicated student of human nature is learning just how fascinating your subject can really be! Are you ready?

Chapter 1: Learning to Listen—To Everything

If your aim is to become an expert at observing and understanding social dynamics, then it makes sense that your first task is to get really good at simply *seeing* what's in front of you.

This may sound a bit strange—aren't we always observing people? The answer is, not really.

Most of us allow enormous amounts of useful social information to completely wash over us. Maybe we're more worried about how we appear to others to focus on how they appear to us, or maybe we're simply distracted. Maybe we've mistakenly taken the social interaction as a chance to express ourselves rather than to appreciate others. Whatever the case, the truth is that you may be surprised at what you start to notice when you pay close, strategic attention to the social world around you.

What goes on inside people's worlds is hidden from us. What we *can* see, however, is the outward expression of that inner world.

We can read not just body language, facial expression, appearance, and language choice, but the unfolding social dynamic, which is bigger than just a single individual. In other words, social interactions and relationships themselves can be a rich source of information, and we can learn to read them just the same as we can read a lifted eyebrow, a symbol on a necklace, or a nervous laugh.

People Watching

The human body is a "communication device," at least according to computer scientist David Fouhey. If we really want to understand the many messages it sends, we need to pay attention to how that device actually works in its natural environment. Psychologists Kerri Johnson and Maggie Shiffar would agree and believe that the human body is probably the most important stimulus that triggers our judgment and perception of a person.

You can think of the information we gather from reading the body as an ancient and built-in communication system that evolved long before our more formal ability to use language and symbols. Learning to read people, then, is simply a matter of shifting your perspective so that you **see people *themselves* as a form of language.**

In just the same way as we can read a sentence and put the letters together to form words, and the words together to form sentences, and understand the sentences as part of a bigger narrative, we can do the same with people: The many little clues come together and start to suggest a bigger meaning. We can start to see that cluster of meanings, in its expanded context, interacting with the social environment around it. Reading people can start to feel as fascinating as reading some of the world's great novels!

It's about Attention

It took time to learn to read, and in the same way it will take time to learn to read and understand the vast and complex social landscape you may find yourself in. We will begin our journey with a question of attention—namely, where you focus it. Below we'll look at five different areas that you can zoom in on as you embark on a little people watching. They're inspired by tips from psychologist Susan Krauss Whitbourne.

Identity

It's arguably a skill most teenagers have become world experts at: quickly determining group membership based on appearance. Yes, we shouldn't judge a book by its cover, but the fact is that you can learn a lot about how somebody classifies *themselves* by looking at the "uniform" they wear. Remind yourself that no choice a person makes about their appearance is arbitrary, and that clothing and accessories, being a kind of extension of the body, also send a particular message. What is that message, do you think, and to whom is it sent? Why? Think about:

- Religious markers (like a pentagram on a shirt, a head scarf, a yarmulke)
- Regional markers (local sports regalia, traditional dress, items associated with a place)
- Class markers (items or styles people believe send the message "I'm rich")
- Education (a college shirt, a tweed jacket ... even a cap and gown!)
- Interests and hobbies (a Rasta-style beanie, a band T-shirt, hand-embroidered hair ribbons)

People may carry around a curio from a recent vacation, they may have tattoos (a whole world of meaning), certain clothing logos, fashionable or decidedly unfashionable garments . . . Each of these things is sending a message. For example, what can you "read" in the fact that you see a person carrying around an umbrella on a hot, cloudless summer day?

Self-Esteem

Yes, you guessed it—posture is a big clue to someone's self-esteem. The way someone carries themselves bodily tells you a lot about how they carry themselves through life psychologically and emotionally. A tall posture with upright chin and shoulders held calmly back and down sends an obvious message of confidence and control. Slouching, hunching, and cowering send the opposite message.

Self-esteem manifests in other ways, too. Being exceptionally well-groomed may speak to a degree of vanity and self-absorption, or perhaps it may be compensation for a deeper insecurity. How could you tell? The trick is the rest of the context. If an exquisitely well-groomed person also talks over everyone else, takes up too much room, and starts every sentence with "I," then you know that they are probably quite egotistical, while the well-dressed person who avoids eye contact, mumbles, and shuffles their feet is probably less certain about their worth! When they clutch an expensive designer handbag across their chest, they may be using it as an emotional shield rather than a badge of superiority. In this way, when we read people, we realize that certain things can have more than one meaning—more on this later.

Emotional State

Anxiety is a state of mind, but it is constantly and freely expressed in the way that people move, talk, gesture, and pose. Anxious energy is quick, restless, and uneasy and will show itself as fidgeting, tightness in the face and body, and tense/shallow breathing—which means a thin, rushed, and choked voice. Distractable people who allow their gaze, their speech, or their limbs to wander all over the place in a disorganized way are showing you quite clearly what it's like on the inside of their minds: chaotic! This is the person who might be carelessly and untidily dressed or making clumsy mistakes.

Likewise, depression is expressed in all areas as slowness and heaviness. Slumped shoulders, downcast mouth and eyes, slow, low voices, and a gait that lacks any purpose or direction speak to a person who is finding life heavy. People who are depressed may lose interest in personal grooming, may be slow to react and speak, and may move with little enthusiasm. They may show visible—if subtle—signs of self-neglect, like stained or holey clothing, bitten nails, or clothing that is not keeping them properly warm or dry.

Agreeableness

For psychologists, this "big five" personality trait is what most of us would simply call being *nice*. Friendly, warm, accommodating people try to get along with others and are decidedly not rebellious, argumentative, or contrary. Can you really see such a personality trait in a person just by looking at them? Yes!

Notice how a person is holding the door open for someone, how they subtly change their language when children are around, whether they share, or simply how they adopt open expressions and body language when listening to others.

The person who is stomping around without concern for the people he's bumping into, or the person who is oblivious to those he might be inconveniencing, may obviously be lower on agreeableness, as will the person who is wearing an obscene shirt (or no shirt?) in public or who makes a point of wearing white to a wedding or red to a funeral. All these little gestures and acts send signals of noncompliance, inconsiderateness to others, or perhaps outright malice.

Extroversion or Introversion

Finally, one fascinating area to focus on is the degree of extroversion or introversion a person is communicating by their appearance, body language, and actions. We tend to think of extroversion as a person who simply talks a lot, but really, an extrovert's orientation is about their relationship to the environment: An extrovert will seek out and maintain engagement with the world and other people, whereas introverts tend not to seek out this kind of stimulation, even though they may respond to it.

The woman who is quick to make eye contact, happy to start up a conversation, and at ease with getting up and moving around the room to get involved in everything is likely more extroverted. An extrovert may "project" all aspects of themselves more noticeably into the environment. Their clothing may be "louder" and literally take up more room, they may seek out and enjoy attention, speak clearly and boldly, even be more tactile with people.

An introvert may be just as friendly and warm, but they may be the one perched in the corner, not moving much, and not instigating anything in particular. There may be other things about them that are "quieter," from the colors they're wearing to the volume of their voice to the topics they choose to talk about.

How to Start People Watching

Ready to put your own attention to the test and see what you notice? Find a good place to people watch (an airport, a busy café, a bus station, or a college campus) and simply watch (politely and respectfully) as people pass by.

Now, you're not trying to craft elaborate stories about these strangers or make judgmental speculations about them. **Try to simply observe.** Then, according to the above areas of focus, challenge yourself to "read" people in a more strategic way. You can even bring a notebook with you if you like.

1. How do you think this person identifies themselves?
2. What do you think their current level of self-esteem is?
3. What is their emotional state?
4. Do they seem more or less agreeable?
5. Are they more extroverted or introverted?

Of course, you may spot someone and instantly have a feeling or intuition about them. But our goal is not mere guesswork at this stage; instead, see if you can identify exactly what it was that made you jump to the conclusion you did. We all come with our own prejudices and biases, but it takes careful and deliberate attention to start reading people in a more strategic way.

The Four Cs of Body Language

In this chapter, we're going to dig a little deeper into body language and exactly how to read the seemingly infinite number of ways people can move their bodies and faces as they go about their day.

Let's say you were people watching one day, and you saw a young couple (*are* they a couple?) standing on the sidewalk, having a conversation. The man has one arm propped up against the wall very close to the woman's face and is leaning closely in toward her. She is standing with her back to the wall, looking up at him with crossed arms and knitted brows. She keeps gesturing off to the left at something else, and he is nodding as he listens to her speak. He's frowning too.

Now the question is, what is this situation about? How shall we interpret all this body language?

The good news is that our ability to read body language clues is a primal survival skill that has been with us since caveman days. We never need to learn people-reading from scratch! A Princeton study suggested that people take just one hundred milliseconds to come to a first impression about people (Willis and Todorov 2016). In other words, your gut feeling about a person or situation is lightning fast and likely pretty accurate—after all, it evolved precisely to protect you and helped your ancestors to quickly determine who was friend or foe.

That said, quick does not necessarily mean accurate, and in fact we may err on the side of snap judgments that detect more threat than there really is. Returning to our example, what did you think of the young couple in the street? Conventional body language advice will tell you that when a woman has her back to a wall and a man is leaning in close, "caging" her in with one arm, he is flirting (aggressively, at that). We have also all been told that crossing your arms means that you're angry, as does frowning. Conclusion? The interaction is a broadly negative one, with a man pestering a woman and her sending a clear message that she isn't interested.

The very moment you've come to that conclusion, however, you continue to watch as the woman bursts into tears, leans in, and gives the man an enormous hug, burying her face in his chest. He pats her head and gives it a kiss, still frowning. You see all at once that she is upset about something completely different, and that this man is listening closely and then comforting her. It turns out, all the signs and clues you read before meant something completely different from what you thought!

The "four Cs" can help us become better at reading body language and avoid making these kinds of common and very understandable errors. Let's take a closer look.

Context

No single piece of body language happens in a vacuum. It is always connected to a broader set of circumstances, to other people, and to the surrounding environment. So, don't merely look at the body language signal in isolation, but consider the context it appears in.

To return to our example, the young woman could be crossing her arms simply because it's a cold day. She may be frowning because the sun is in her eyes or because she's angry at a rude altercation she's just had with a stranger (that is, the thing she keeps gesturing toward). In the same way as the word "bank" can have two different meanings depending on the rest of the sentence ("Bank of America" versus "bank of the river"), so, too, can each gesture mean something different depending on what's surrounding it.

As you observe people, gather as much data as possible and avoid zooming in on just one or two pixels of the image you see—you might risk losing resolution on the bigger picture that way! Try to keep in mind recent events, the time (hour, day of the week, season, etc.), the surrounding environment, and the social situation that the body language signal occurred in.

One final thing to consider is that the person sending the signal is themselves a "context." You may not always know a person and the idiosyncratic ways that they communicate nonverbally. Remember that you are always observing a unique, specific individual who has their own distinctive patterns and perspectives.

Clusters

A useful concept in the art of body language reading is to **think in clusters—i.e., group of signals rather than just one or two signals**. For example, many people have been told that a woman touching and playing with her hair is being flirtatious. Now, if a woman is saying, "Sorry, I'm not interested," and she is scowling and turning her body away from you *and* she's wearing a wedding ring...chances are that the brief moment she touched her hair was not flirtation!

Try to identify clusters of signals that all suggest similar messages, or the same signal sent repeatedly and consistently. One signal means little, but with five or more you can start to make more accurate guesses. Clusters can help you make sense of ambiguous signals (for example, talking quickly and breathlessly could show anxiety or excitement—the other signals will help you discern which).

Sometimes, the fact that a signal occurs plenty of times is precisely the reason you can discount it as meaningful in any way. For example, you may wrongly conclude that someone is flirting with you simply because you haven't observed their behavior over the long term with other people—if you had, you might have noticed that this person pretty much "flirts" with everyone. In other words, that's just their baseline.

Congruence

As we noted earlier, all behavior and communication happen in context. It's done for a reason. We saw how a person who dresses in white to someone else's wedding may be showing signs of low agreeableness, but it's not that a white dress in itself *means* disagreeableness. After all, the bride is engaging in the exact same behavior, and if the guest wore white on any other day, it wouldn't mean much.

Congruence is about drawing our attention to the fit of certain signals and behavior with everything else in the context. If someone is behaving in ways that make sense considering the context, then we can assume that the behavior is not saying anything special. For example, it's hot so you wear less clothing. But what about the person who has chosen to wear very little clothing in cold weather? It is not the clothing that is sending the message but the *incongruence* of their actions with their environment and context. That is what a good body language reader will notice and be interested in.

There can also be a lack of congruence within a person. If someone's words and their actions are not in congruence, it suggests some kind of misalignment within them, or even deception. When verbal language says one thing and non-verbal another, be curious about what the mismatch means (and usually, it's the non-verbal communication that's closer to the truth).

Finally, look for incongruence with others or within group dynamics. Notice when one person in a group appears to be on a completely different emotional wavelength from everyone else, or is seemingly behaving out of step with them in some way. What does that incongruence suggest?

Culture

You've probably already guessed that culture is a major part of how we interpret and make sense of social signals. **Body language is innate and has a biological basis, but it's also heavily shaped and influenced by culture.** Different groups of people all have quite different ideas about personal space, touching, smiling, and what is considered rude or friendly.

In Arab cultures, men easily hold hands with one another to demonstrate their friendship, while in other cultures this may be coded as sexual. In some Asian cultures a big smile may be employed to diffuse tension and relieve awkwardness, whereas Western people would consider smiling during an uncomfortable moment rude and inappropriate. The rules around personal space, privacy, and speaking volume in a crowded and industrialized city may be very different from those in a rural area, and certain hand signs and gestures in one place may mean something completely different in another.

When someone touches you while speaking, such as casually brushing your arm or sitting closely, it often signifies attraction or friendliness. Cultural norms, however, play a significant role in interpreting such gestures. Personal space is valued in Western cultures like New York or London, and excessive physical contact may be seen as intrusive. How awkward this would seem would depend very much on where you were!

How can you apply the four Cs as you continue to develop your observation and people-watching skills? The next time you are observing a person, a social situation, or even a single behavior, ask yourself:

1. What is the context that this occurs in, and how does that context give meaning to this signal?
2. Are there any other behaviors that send the same/similar message?
3. Is the signal at odds somehow with the context, the person themselves, or other people? What does that incongruence suggest?
4. Does this behavior have any particular meaning in the cultural context?

Remembering the four Cs will help you avoid some of the most common pitfalls of learning to read social cues.

How to Read the Voice

The voice can be thought of as a part of the body. It is created when the body shapes and expels air in its own distinctive way, and its expression heavily depends on the body it originates from. The voice is made out of breath, and our emotional state, our health, our age, and our gender can all impact how that breath flows through us. Thus, when you're hearing someone's voice, you are hearing what may arguably be the most authentic expression of their being. In other words, it's worth paying attention to!

The trick, of course, is to realize that listening to a person doesn't just mean listening to the *words* they say (although we will explore that a little later on!). There is a nonverbal or "paralingual" aspect to the voice, too, and it may reveal more information about a person than even their facial expression. There is a reason that people sometimes describe harmony and understanding as "resonating" with another person—this auditory clue lets you know that there are complex links between empathy, understanding, and hearing a person's voice.

We now know that human beings learn to understand and empathize with one another by unconsciously and subtly mirroring their facial expressions. The idea is that when we can feel another person's experience in our own bodies, it allows us to really understand and connect with that person (Dimberg et al. 2000).

What's interesting is that this same phenomenon may occur when we hear people's voices. A study by Michael Kraus (titled "Voice-Only Communication Enhances Empathic Accuracy") suggests that **our sense of hearing may be even more powerful at detecting emotion than our sense of sight**. The study found that people were better at detecting others' emotions when they heard voice alone compared to only seeing their face or seeing their face and hearing their voices at the same time. You read that right: They found that emotional understanding (i.e., empathy) was best when voice was the *only* available cue.

Kraus's guess is that when we listen only to the voice, our full attention can focus on the subtleties in voice quality. Particularly on the phone, you may be more aware of changes in breathing pattern, pauses, or shifts in tone or pitch. Of course, this finding doesn't help us much when we consider how to become better at reading social cues and understanding social dynamics, but it does tell us that if we selectively pay attention to the voice, there is plenty of opportunity for discerning how a person really feels, and thus having real empathy for them.

Your ability to detect the nuances and subtleties in voice is there; it just needs you to acknowledge and develop it. Today, sadly, much of our communication is tech-mediated, and we are "social" without ever encountering one another in any kind of embodied way. One lesson we can take from Kraus's study and others like it is that we lose a wealth of embodied and nonverbal information when we make communication digital-only.

Some of the ways we both express and receive paralingual information are deeply wired into our unconscious minds. For example, some anthropologists and evolutionary psychologists claim that men often lower the pitch of their voices as well as the volume (loudness) to send an unconscious signal that they are larger than average (because we associate big voices with big bodies). For men, this subtle communication is used to send signals of high mate value to women, but also to communicate social dominance to other men. By the same token, women may increase the pitch of their voice, especially during ovulation, in a bid to signal their attractiveness, youth, and fertility.

All of this is to say that sometimes we cannot help what we express through our voice. Psychologist Paul Ekman believes that sometimes our deeper emotions are revealed through "leakage" in our voice—and you can hear all this if you know what to listen for.

Karl Scherer works at the Affective Sciences Center at the University of Geneva and explains how we can listen to speech according to a few of its physical characteristics:

- Frequency (pitch—i.e., whether high or low)

- Intensity (loudness level)
- Variation in frequency (dynamism, i.e.—switching between high and low. With low variation, you have a monotonous voice)
- Articulation rate (rapidity or speed)

Certain emotions express themselves as follows:

Stress, fear, or anxiety: Increased intensity/loudness of speech and increased frequency/pitch of speech. A person may speak a lot, and sometimes quite quickly. Listen for breath that seems to "run out" before the end of the sentence, gasping, or a tight-sounding voice—all signs that a person is currently tense and breathing in a shallow or constricted way—i.e., stressed.

Anger: As with stress and anxiety, angry people speak with greater intensity/volume and frequency/pitch, or they may show frequency variability. Listen also for increased articulation rate (speaking rapidly) but also greater emphasis, enunciation, and clarity around particular points.

Sadness: Everything decreased: intensity, frequency, frequency variability, and articulation rate. Depressed or demotivated people often speak slowly, quietly, with little dynamism or variation in their voice.

Joy, excitement, and happiness: Everything increased: intensity and frequency, frequency variability, articulation rate. Joyful people's speech is "colorful," bright, and interesting.

Boredom: Decreased frequency variability and articulation rate. Speech that reflects little change in speed, tone, or volume has become very one-note and signals a lack of interest and boredom.

Of course, out in the real world, people may display an extremely wide range of complex emotions, including very neutral ones. As you listen to someone speak, it can be difficult to listen to the quality of the voice itself because you will most likely be listening carefully to the words as well!

As they speak, first just try to get an overall impression of their vocal expression. Then, later, you can start to zoom in on the finer details (without zoning out and missing what they're saying, of course!).

Here are a few more tips and tricks for improving your ability to really listen to people's voices:

1. **Listen to Tone, Pitch, and Volume:** Pay close attention to how the tone and pitch of the voice varies, and ask what this might be communicating. A sudden

change in pitch could suggest a change in interest levels. A sudden drop in volume could signal the revelation of a secret or an invitation to more closeness (because what happens when people whisper? Others have to lean in more closely to hear them!). Of course, the four Cs will help you interpret these vocal changes in context.

2. **Notice Vocal Quality:** Evaluate the overall quality of the voice. For example, if a colleague's voice is shaky during a stressful presentation, they may be feeling nervous or anxious. On the other hand, if you hear a parent speaking with a calm and steady voice, they are likely conveying reassurance and safety to a child. As you listen, remember that voice is made of breath, so pay attention to how people are breathing and you will gain an insight into how they are feeling.

3. **Identify Vocal Bursts:** Recognize spontaneous vocal bursts like sighs, gasps, or exclamations. For instance, if you hear a sharp intake of breath when someone receives unexpected news, they might be expressing surprise or concern. Similarly, if you hear a contented "Ahh!" while someone

discusses a favorite hobby, they are likely showing genuine pleasure and enthusiasm. Vocal signals could be more subtle than this, of course. Listen for little laughs, throat-clearing, or any other little sounds—they are like emotional punctuation!

4. **Practice!** You can really develop your listening muscle by regularly listening to podcasts, interviews, or other vocal presentations—especially ones where you can't see the person's face or body. Pause now and again to make observations about what you hear and what these observations may mean. One interesting exercise is to briefly mimic the person speaking—and then see how *you* feel. We'll expand on this idea below.

Listen to Your Own Voice as Well

Listening to how your vocal expression changes can yield interesting insights into other people. Jean-Julien Aucouturier and his colleagues conducted a study that had them concluding that people tend to make inferences about how we feel based on the quality of our own voice. What this means is that if you want to know how you feel about someone, listen to their voice but also to yours as you speak to them. **You may be reacting unconsciously and automatically in ways that tell you a lot about what is unfolding in the interaction.**

Have you ever noticed how you sometimes match your facial expression to the people you watch on TV? The same thing happens with vocal expression. As you listen, you may unconsciously mirror another person's way of speaking. This is why your own voice can actually be a useful source of information to pay attention to. If, for example, you notice that your own voice has risen in pitch and seems a little more breathless, become curious why. Might *they* be feeling a bit anxious?

Interpreting Smiles

Even the least emotionally intelligent among us knows that a smile doesn't automatically mean that a person is "happy." In fact, many of us know very well that some of the creepiest fictional villains are those with distorted smiles and maniacal laughs! A smile is certainly a form of communication; after all, we all smile on cue when someone brings out a camera and tells us to say cheese. Yet smiles are also a spontaneous and natural expression of joy and friendliness.

In this section, we're going to be considering how to read a smile, and that starts with the acknowledgment that there are many different *types* of smiles. Have you ever looked at a big group photo and noticed how some of the people's smiles somehow seem more natural and "real" than others? While everyone may seemingly be doing the same thing with their faces, it's almost as though the "fake" smiles actually annoy you, or perhaps make you suspicious.

Maybe you never even noticed yourself thinking this way, but merely concluded that there were just certain people you liked and didn't like, certain people who were more trustworthy, more attractive, and so on, without really thinking about *why* you felt that way.

The truth is all of us are constantly analyzing and interpreting the tiniest of expressions in other people's faces at all times, making rapid and largely unconscious determinations about who we are looking at, whether we like them, and importantly whether we can trust them or not.

The trouble with reading smiles is that the face is capable of two parallel processes: It can reveal natural, spontaneous, and genuine feeling . . . but it can also deliberately and consciously display an expression chosen for some particular purpose (i.e., it's possible to fake it).

This is not necessarily the deception it sounds like, of course. Dana Howard and colleagues (2018) found that smiling serves a valid social role and that we perceive a smile as a kind of reward that draws us closer to people, thus strengthening social cohesion. People who smile on purpose are trying to leverage this natural process, in effect communicating the message "I want you to see that I'm happy. I'm a friend. I want you to be my friend. I'm likeable and I like you." When people view you this way, they are far more likely to want to help you and work with you. In other words, **smiling is pro-social behavior** that really pays off.

As you can guess, there are other functions a smile can serve. We smile to show that we are relaxed, that a temporary social snag has been overcome, that we sympathize, or that we recognize some level of shared kinship . . . but we can also smile as a threat, as a sign of dominance, mocking, or even contempt.

Welsh researcher Magdalena Rychlowska et al. (2017) used a complex method of observation and modeling to classify smiles, of which she found three distinct functional categories.

- **Reward smile.** This is the smile made when you want to send a message of positive feedback, appreciation, or recognition. You can identify this smile by the slightly upturned corners of the mouth and a corresponding eyebrow lift—there may also be little dimples at the side of the smile. It tends to be symmetrical. If you want to know what this kind of smile looks like, imagine you are talking to a cute baby or puppy and you want to convince them to smile back or like you—the smile you have on your face will be a reward smile!
- **Affiliative smile.** This is the smile that sends a message of friendship and liking. It's characterized by pressing the lips together and also by the same little dimples made by the reward smile. It tends to be spread wider and thinner than the reward smile and usually shows no teeth. This smile makes an appearance when people want to acknowledge a social bond they share, or else demonstrate tolerance or fondness. When that cute baby or puppy does something naughty, you might show them an affiliative smile.

- **Dominance smile.** Finally, a smile where the upper lip is raised (which lifts the cheeks up high) and the nose appears a little wrinkled—almost like a sneer. Confusingly, the cheeks may be lifted quite high compared to the other types, but a dominance smile tends not to be symmetrical and may "fade" slowly into a less appealing expression. These smiles are used to establish and acknowledge social hierarchies. Imagine this smile used on a sports pitch, in a boardroom, or in a complex social setting where people of different rank and status are interacting.

If you were to bear all this in mind and return to the group photo we mentioned earlier, you may now be able to put a finger on all those smiles that appeared less-than-sincere to you. Most likely, the fake smiles are those where the eyes are more open and the contractions and indentations in the face appear more "snarl-like," or else they lack the dimples or upturned corners of the reward or affiliative smile.

When people are instructed to smile, or they know they should, they tend to make only superficial movements associated with smiling—they may mechanically raise the corners of their mouths and show their teeth.

What they tend *not* to do is crinkle up their eyes or form dimples.

Most photographers know that when people smile naturally, there is overall much less tension in the face, and the smile erupts over the features all at once and quite quickly. The smile "reaches the eyes," and they close a little. A more considered and deliberate smile, on the other hand, will be slower to form and more effortful—i.e., you may be able to see the muscular tension in the cheeks and mouth. The eyes may stay relatively more open and alert.

Rychlowska and colleagues identified three broad smile types, but there are probably far more types. You can likely think of people who smile when they're nervous and anxious (perhaps the grin is paired with downward sloping eyebrows and the corners of the mouth are spread but not really lifted upward?) or when they're feeling wistful and a little sad (the lips pursed inward) or shocked (a smile paired with a more open mouth and lifted eyebrows).

When it comes to reading smiles, all the same body language rules apply:

- Pay attention to context—is this person smiling while everyone else isn't, or vice versa? Why should that be?
- Pay attention to clusters—how often do you see the person smile and what tends to provoke it or make it fade away? If a person smiles and makes eye contact when they tell you a particular piece of information, become curious about the significance of that piece of information—the smile is telling you that the speaker thinks it's important.
- Pay attention to congruence—is the person saying they're miserable while smiling? Are they sitting stony-faced in a hilarious comedy show? Why?
- Finally, culture may play the biggest role of all. Smiles mean very different things to different groups of people. For some it signals respect and politeness; for others it's a gesture of intimacy, flirtation, appeasement, or even simple-mindedness! Bear in mind that smiles may be the most gendered of all nonverbal expressions, and smiles mean different things for men than they do women.
- Even if you're having trouble spotting the four Cs, simply notice whether a smile *feels* real or forced. If it's not a natural smile, ask yourself what the most obvious reason for

the smile may be, then gather more information.

As you get better at people watching, keep reminding yourself that a smile is often a piece of deliberate communication in just the same way as a word, gesture, or facial expression is. Ask yourself: **"If this smile could talk, what would it say?"** The more you observe others this way, the more you'll see that it's as though each smile is totally and completely unique.

"I want you to think I'm polite."
"Back off."
"Aren't I pretty?"
"This is boring, huh?"
"Hehe . . . good one."
"Wow, you're hot stuff."
"There, there . . . it will be all right."
"Ha! Serves him right, the big idiot."
"I love you."
"I love this cake."
"Please don't look at me. Please don't look at me . . ."

In fact, a fun exercise is to read through the above smile "messages" and imagine that you are an actor or actress tasked with communicating the message with nothing but your smile. As you do so, notice what your own face is doing. Notice in particular what your mouth, eyes, and cheeks are doing. You may even look in a mirror and see what differences you can discern between, for example, an embarrassed versus a flirtatious versus a vengeful smile. The more you are able to tune into these slight nuances in yourself, the better you will be able to spot them in other people.

Summary:

- Be honest: How good of a judge of character are you? To become a better people-reader requires more than just reading about people; we need to learn to be open-minded, willing to learn, and practical.
- What goes on inside people's worlds is hidden from us. What we *can* see, however, is the outward expression of that inner world. Our first task is to become excellent observers.
- The body itself is a kind of communication and can be read. Try people watching. There are four broad areas we can focus our attention on: identity, self-esteem, emotional state, agreeableness, and introversion/extroversion. Observe immediate appearance to give clues about the group that person considers themselves part of. Observe posture and grooming for clues to overall self-esteem.

Look for speed, chaos, and tension to suggest anxiety, or slowness and heaviness to suggest depression.
- Always keep in mind the four Cs of body language. When you notice a signal, consider its context, clusters of other signals, congruence of that signal with other signals, and the cultural setting.
- Remember that no single piece of body language happens in a vacuum, and that behavioral signals are best interpreted in groups and patterns. Always strive to see the bigger picture.
- To read the voice, pay attention to its tone, pitch, volume, modulation, variation, and overall expression—regardless of the words spoken. Likewise with smiles, be aware that some are genuine, and some aren't.

Chapter 2: How to Read the Room

In the previous chapter, we considered the fine art of people watching and learned how to start developing our powers of social observation. By noticing context, clusters of behaviors, environmental congruence, and the overall cultural setting, we learned to deploy our attention more deliberately to all the ways that people express their identity, mood, overall personality, and self-esteem in nonverbal ways.

In this chapter, we're going to take a step away from being purely detached observers and start to explore ways to read social dynamics even as we ourselves are a part of them. Knowing how to "read the room" is actually a complicated set of many different abilities—some of which may come easy to you, and some of which may seem totally alien. Let's explore a few.

Knowing When the Conversation Is Over

We'll start with a simple one: knowing when someone is interested in engaging . . . and when they're ready for the conversation to end.

If most of us are honest, a big part of the anxiety of social interaction is never knowing how someone *really* feels about you. People may be polite or fake it to the degree that it's difficult to know whether they are genuinely interested or not. This poses a catch-22 situation: If we are doing something wrong socially, others may not actually signal this to us and so we may blindly carry on doing it. Because most people naturally don't want to appear rude or reject us outright, we are ultimately robbed of any corrective feedback they could give us, and so may have a quite poor idea of how we are perceived in social settings.

That said, the problem can also go the other way—people, having themselves been rejected and wanting to avoid the same, may err on the side of being a little cool when it comes to displaying their own interest. They may send vague clues (or none at all) when in fact they are very interested in you.

Confusing, right?

Let's be honest: Human beings are messy and confusing at the best of times, and even the most socially adept person will occasionally meet someone who doesn't like or understand them. This is important to reiterate: *It's normal.* Nevertheless, within the normal bounds, there is plenty of room to learn to more accurately detect when people are genuinely having a nice time interacting with you.

Social researchers Fichten et al. (1992) were fascinated by the "mixed signals" phenomenon and conducted plenty of interesting research where they observed and interviewed men and women in social situations—both in everyday and dating conversations. They wanted to know what we all want to know: How do people behave when they're interested in someone, and how can you distinguish them from those who are disinterested but trying to be polite?

Well, their results led them to conclude that there were several verbal and nonverbal cues signaling when a person was ready to end the conversation. These are included below with some additional advice, but bear in mind that wanting the conversation to be over is not automatically the same as not being interested (more on that later).

Verbal Cues

Listen carefully for language that appears to be concluding, wrapping up, or somehow verbally putting an end to things. Responses may become shorter and more closed (so there is less for you to pick up and elaborate on), and there may also be a change in topics—i.e., the conversation content seems to become a little lighter or more superficial.

An interested conversation partner will be showing signs of wanting to keep the conversation going—open-ended questions, engaging comments, even compliments. Crucially, a person can signal their interest even as they end the conversation—for example, by asking for your number or by outright expressing a wish or making a plan/invitation to see you again.

A disinterested person will do the opposite and brush off any suggestion of the conversation/interaction continuing in the future, and their responses will be rushed or short or will demonstrate a slow shifting of attention away from the interaction to something else (the person is already mentally preparing for what they're going to do next).

Be wary of interpreting any one signal as definitive, however. For example, a woman may agree to give you her number and do so quickly, but closely observing other cues will reveal that she has done so in a bid to finally break free (after giving you a fake number). As always, remember the four Cs and consider what a signal means given context clues.

Other ways people can verbally communicate a desire to disengage:

- Summarizing language: "Well, it's been such a nice chat."
- Resorting to generic pleasantries: "Well, it was really nice to see you."
- Departure statements: "Well, it's getting late..."
- Mentioning other activities elsewhere: "Wow, I've got a lot to do this afternoon."
- Making plans: "We should catch up again soon."
- Pre-emptive warning and justification: "I have to pick up the kids, so I can only chat for a moment..."

If the person says any of the above, you can take it as a pretty clear sign that they are ready for the conversation to end. Continuing to talk at this point or (heaven forbid) making moves to expand and deepen the conversation will be met with annoyance and will eventually create rupture and disharmony in that relationship. Imagine that once a verbal statement of a desire to disconnect has been made, a bomb timer has suddenly been set, and you have twenty seconds to get out of the building!

People will often couch verbal statements like these in lots of politeness, but it's a mistake to latch on to the politeness rather than receive the underlying message: The conversation is over. For example, someone may say, "I've got to get going now, which is a pity because I've really loved hearing all about your time in Greece. You should tell me more about the food when we chat over the weekend..."

Now, while the person is verbally expressing an interest in hearing more and how it's a pity they can't, it would be wrong to reply with, "Oh, the food! I didn't tell you. We had this amazing meal on our first evening there, did I mention? It was this little mom-and-pop restaurant, a really charming place..."

Nonverbal Cues

If you've spent some time people watching, you may have noticed when someone is clearly disinterested in a conversation and is not paying much attention. From afar, you might have even wondered how it could be obvious to *you*, and yet the other person in the conversation seemingly continued to talk, oblivious. How could that be?

The truth is that **nonverbal signs of disinterest are usually pretty obvious, but we're often simply too self-absorbed to catch them.** We may be worried about how we're coming across, or else so engrossed in communicating our point that we have very little attention left to notice how well that point is being received. Luckily, this is all easily remedied by paying closer attention. If you notice *any* of these signs, immediately back off and see what response you get. If you happen to have read it wrong, the person will do something to continue the conversation. But if you've read their signal right, they'll quickly make their escape.

- Checking their phone (especially if it's more than once)
- Packing away their things or putting on coats and jackets, etc.
- Doing other things as you talk—for example, trying to start a minor chore or surreptitiously doing a small work task
- Fiddling or fidgeting
- Being distracted, having a wandering gaze, or showing increasing attention in things outside the conversation
- Suddenly standing (if they were sitting) or moving a little toward an exit

- Starting another conversation or trying to subtly engage someone else
- Checking their watch or clock
- Any body language that moves them away from you physically
- Yawning, stretching, clapping their hands together, or patting their thighs

The above list is not exhaustive, but all these behaviors share something in common: They signal that the stream of attention that the other person was once sending toward you and the conversation is starting to falter or be directed elsewhere. Watch for these "attentional shifts," especially if they are paired with verbal cues.

Other Cues

All conversations have a natural lifespan. **The fact of a conversation coming to an end is not a sign that anything is wrong or that the other person is not interested.** Sometimes, people who are socially anxious or unconfident in their conversation skills can sense an impending end to a conversation and unconsciously panic, feeling that they are being rejected, or that they need to quickly do something to win back the attention of the other person. They may not even realize that they are responding to signals to end the conversation by doubling down and talking even more. Here are a few things to keep in mind that will help you navigate the ending of a conversation:

- In a very casual group setting, conversations last only around five or ten minutes. They can last longer if both parties are really enjoying it, but unless you see obvious signs of extreme enthusiasm, assume that after ten minutes it's time to chat with someone else.
- Most conversations begin for a particular reason—for example, exchanging information, asking questions, sharing opinions, etc. Once that objective is achieved, it's a good time to move things along. In more casual and free-form settings, it can be harder to know when the conversation has served its purpose, but try to stick to broadly one main topic or theme and then part ways when you feel like it's been exhausted.
- A big clue that the conversation is reaching its natural end is the increasing number of silences. Running out of things to talk about is not unusual and not a sign that anything awkward or unpleasant is going on; it's simply a sign to *allow* the conversation to come to a close with grace. No need to make it awkward!

Finally, a word of warning. **Generally, people tend to want conversations to last less time across the board.** That means that if you're ever unsure, opt for a shorter conversation rather than a longer one. When it comes to conversation ends in particular, be extra alert to even small signs of disengagement, since most people will tend to downplay or hide their disinterest. Men especially tend to overestimate the interest of women in romantic settings (Haselton and Buss 2000; Henningsen and Henningsen 2010), so factor this in.

Cooperative Overlapping

Everyone knows that interrupting people as they speak is the height of rudeness, right?

Well, maybe and maybe not. Most of us don't really think about this aspect of social life, but the manner in which people share and take turns with the airspace in a social interaction is itself a powerful message, and a reflection of connection and harmony. Consider the following situations:

- Three older men are sitting around a table, drinking. One is telling an amusing anecdote, but before he is finished speaking, another jumps in and talks over

him. Everyone's attention switches to the second man as he introduces a new topic—which is much like the old topic, except this time the anecdote is about *him*.
- A group of excitable young girls are all having a sleepover and chatting together. It's hard to tell who the main speaker even is, because their speech is constantly overlapping, and there are excited giggles and exclamations throughout.
- Two people in a work context are puzzling over an email. One is talking when the other interrupts to say, "Wait, are we talking about Mr. Jones himself or Jones Wholesale?" The other answers the question, saying, "No, the company Jones Wholesale. You know. The people who sell the, the . . ." The other person interrupts here and finishes the sentence for them, saying, "Plastic ducting. Yeah, I know them. They're an old client."

Now, all of the examples above are considered interruptions, but you can probably tell that they are very, very different from one another. In previous chapters, we've driven home the point that no single behavior, word, or expression categorically means something, and in the same way, interrupting is never conclusively "good" or "bad." Rather, **it's the function that the interruption plays, the**

context it occurs in, and the ultimate effect it has on the interaction itself that matters. Let's take a closer look.

Sociologists and anthropologists actually use the term "cooperative overlapping" to speak about conversational behavior that is not what most of us think of when we hear the word *interrupt*. How can we tell the difference? Well, merely overlapping speech does not indicate much. Instead, it's a question of whether the interrupter is doing so to cooperate with, or compete with, the original speaker.

Returning to our three examples, it should be clear that the man in the first example is interrupting for the purpose of grabbing attention for himself, stealing "the floor," and perhaps even trying to dominate the first speaker. In the second example, however, the young girls are constantly interrupting each other not to compete, but to cooperate and to mutually participate in a kind of group conversation. Their interjections are supportive and enthusiastic. They're there to contribute more energy and connection, not take away. Their interruptions are more like the person who yells out "Amen!" in a rousing church service or who exclaims "Really?!" at the juiciest part of the story you're telling.

Finally, the third example is cooperative but in a different way—both speakers take turns interrupting one another, but the overall aim is to support the emerging conversation between them and keep it flowing well. If you've ever struggled to remember a name or detail, and someone stepped in to quickly help you out, they were interrupting—but in the nicest way possible!

As we'll see in a later chapter, mirroring, reflecting, and paraphrasing the stories other people tell is a great way to demonstrate our listening and show empathy. We are like the backup singers supporting the main act and, in essence, helping people tell their stories.

Deborah Tannen was the first to introduce the term "cooperative overlapping" in her 1984 book, *Conversational Style: Analyzing Talk Among Friends*. She couldn't help but notice that good friends tended to interrupt one another a whole lot, but that this was a sign of "high involvement style" and not disrespect. This was, she argued, a useful part of active "listenership" and showed engagement and participation. As you can imagine, this paralingual feature of conversations varies widely across cultures and groups.

So, to conclude, according to Julia A. Goldberg, there are two types of interruptions: competitive and cooperative interruptions.

Competitive Interruptions

The overall effect is to disrupt the flow of the conversation and potentially introduce conflict or awkwardness.

Competitive interruptions can be about:

Disagreement—immediately jumping in to share a contrary opinion.
"Floor taking"—the topic remains the same but the spotlight switches to center a different speaker (as in our example above).
Topic change—the interrupter forcefully changes the topic.
Tangentialization—interjecting to sum up what the current speaker is saying in order to hurry them along and end their turn (slightly softer version of changing the topic, not unlike the concluding/departing statements of people who want a conversation to end).

Cooperative Interruptions

The overall effect is to sustain, support, and encourage the flow of the conversation. Rather than to subvert the current speaker, take attention away from them, or end their "turn," the interrupter maintains focus and attention on the original speaker and does not wish to undermine them.

Cooperative interruptions can be about:

Agreement—showing agreement, understanding, compliance, or general support for what is being said.
Assistance—the interrupter offers a word, phrase, or idea to help the main speaker share their message more effectively.
Clarification—asking a question to clarify the shared message.

Having shared these two types of interruptions, however, it's worth mentioning that interruptions are classed according to the function they serve in the conversation—and this function will of course be a matter of consensus between the people speaking. A few things to bear in mind:

Rank and relative status: A person in a perceived higher social status who interrupts someone of perceived lower status will more readily be seen as interrupting in a negative way.

Individual preference and style: Culture aside, some people simply have a preference for one or other type of conversation. If two quite different people are trying to communicate, they may need to be aware of their mismatch and adjust accordingly.

Neurodiversity and stress: For some people or during some circumstances, conversational overlapping can be experienced as information overload and can lead to stress, confusion, or irritation.

Formal or informal context: Remembering the four Cs, context matters, and the degree of formality in a social situation often influences how much overlapping people believe is appropriate. Formal settings tend to demand that speakers get more official uninterrupted time, while casual settings can tolerate more disjointed and overlapping conversations.

Their perspective, not yours! Finally, bear in mind that how an interruption is interpreted actually comes down to the original speaker and not the interrupter. For example, you may genuinely feel that your interjection is helpful and supportive, but if for whatever reason the speaker doesn't feel that way, then that is what matters.

Understanding Interruptions in Social Situations

We can also use our understanding of interruptions and conversational overlap as a way to read into a social situation. So, given all the above, use your fledgling people-reading skills to consider the following:

1. A manager asks an employee plenty of questions but keeps cutting them off as soon as they answer. You notice the manager doesn't do this to their superiors, however.
2. Two people are speaking. One keeps interrupting to blurt out supportive and enthusiastic statements, but the other awkwardly stops, believing the listener doesn't want to hear what they have to say. But then the interrupter doesn't rush to fill in that gap. Awkwardness ensues.
3. You notice that a particular person is almost always interrupted by others with tangentialization (i.e., "let's wrap this up") kind of statements. These same people don't appear to interrupt others in the same way.

Knowing what you know now about interruptions, what can you conclude about the overall social dynamics at play in these three situations?

1. Perhaps you can conclude that the manager is power-hungry and enjoys dominating the employee and abusing the power imbalance between them. Why

should they do that? Further observations may help you answer that question!
2. You might decide that the conversation is difficult because the two people involved are very different from one another and are having trouble establishing any kind of empathy or harmony given this mismatch of styles.
3. Initially it appears that others are being rude, but on closer observation you can see that the frequently interrupted person is a rambler who talks too much and doesn't heed cues of disinterest or exhaustion. In other words, the frequent interruptions are a reflection of that person's own habitual conversational style.

Of course, you can use this knowledge to help you become a better conversationalist yourself. The next time you're tempted to butt in and speak over someone, ask if your interjection would help create more flow or stop up the flow. Ask if it would divert attention away from the speaker or sustain attention where it currently is. Ask if your contribution would add to and strengthen the message being shared or steer attention away from or outright contradict it. Your answers will tell you a lot!

Six Clues to Character

So far, you've learned how to read things that most people don't know are "readable" in social interactions. You might have a new insight into what awkward silences mean in an interaction, as well as what to make of those times when there is seemingly too much talking all at once!

But by now you're also probably wondering what things you can observe and interpret to help you better grasp not only the social dynamic you're witnessing, but the character and personality of the individuals involved.

Susan Engel, a psychologist from Williams College, suggests that understanding someone's development is sometimes like reading a crystal ball, but it's never a complete mystery. What's more, with practice you only become better and better, and soon you may find yourself automatically understanding and predicting people's behavior based on seemingly small pieces of information.

Engel outlined six areas or domains across which you could observe a person's traits:

1. Intelligence
2. Drive
3. Sociability

4. Capacity for intimacy
5. Happiness
6. Goodness

Like many trait psychologists like her, Engel believes that the more fundamental personality traits tend to develop early in human beings and remain stable throughout the life cycle. They also tend to manifest themselves in consistent ways, meaning that you can predict who someone is at a character level, and therefore predict their future behavior simply by observing what they do in the present.

Again, we'll share the caveat that "reading" people is more of an art than an exact science—and is influenced, of course, by our own character. We will master the art of people-reading quicker if we can understand and remove our own biases, expectations, and assumptions from the picture first!

Here's a question for you: **How well do you truly understand the *character* of the people closest to you?** You might know a little about their habits and interests, but do you know what they're really made of and how they will respond to opportunities, challenges, or the unknown?

Many of us think about whether we like or get along with someone, without really asking what their character is—i.e., their deeper nature and more stable tendencies. Consequently, we may be surprised to later learn that they are not as committed to relationships as we had hoped, they are stronger and more resilient than we guessed, or they are more moral and upstanding in tough times than anyone would have predicted.

How much easier would your life be if you could more quickly and more accurately read people on this deeper, more fundamental level?

Engel's book *Red Flags or Red Herrings? Predicting Who Your Child Will Become* explains how to read and interpret behavior in even young children—in whom she claims the seeds of character are already planted.

Engle emphasizes that our intuitions about these kinds of things are not necessarily correct either. For example, people who are shy or quiet are not necessarily less happy, those who win prizes as kids aren't necessarily destined for success as adults, and people who make frequent mistakes and often change their minds are not necessarily unintelligent.

Let's explore each arena a little more closely.

Intelligence

What constitutes intelligence? Well, this is a big question that we won't attempt to answer here, but there are of course multiple components: Intelligence is about memory, executive functioning, the ability to process data, synthesize, create, find patterns, make predictions, and solve problems, to name just a few of its features.

What clues can you observe that hint at a person's intelligence?

It's not a *what* so much as a *how*—**look closely at how a person thinks** (not necessarily what they think). Do they weigh up pros and cons, break things into parts and then reassemble them, look for themes and patterns, and ask thoughtful questions? You're looking for the ability to handle complexity, for cognitive flexibility, and for clarity and creativity of thought.

Notice whether people are able to learn—i.e., adapt to new information from their environment—this, after all, may be the whole point of intelligence in the first place! On the other hand, a person who cannot adapt or adjust according to new feedback is demonstrating a lack of intelligence.

Other clues: Look for "quickness" either in speech or thought, as well as humor, wit, and nonconventionality. Intelligent people are also very capable of taking on different perspectives and shifting their view on a topic. Pay attention to this in conversations—is the other person able to entertain new ideas you put to them, or do they simply repeat what they already know?

Drive

This concerns ambition, passion, perseverance, goal setting, and a kind of go-getter attitude. There are different ways to define this, but it's ultimately a question of determination to strive toward and succeed at what you find valuable.

You will recognize people high in this trait by their energy and effort. They tend to have an independent streak and are quite organized, focused, and hardworking—sometimes to the extreme point of obsession. People lower on this trait may pursue goals but with far less urgency and heat and are happier to let things unfold as they will.

One big clue to drive and ambition is to **notice how a person speaks about problems and obstacles in their lives**. You may even have the opportunity to watch them overcome a hurdle in real life. Do they immediately get fired up and start making plans to get around the problem (high drive), or do they shrug their shoulders, get angry, or resort to blame (lower drive)?

Happiness

Here, Engel is not talking about the momentary feelings of joy or satisfaction that come and go over the course of a day, but rather the *capacity* to find enjoyment and contentment in life in general. Some people are able to be happy in life regardless of what happens to them, while others find it difficult even when circumstances are seemingly perfect.

There are countless ways to think about happiness, but Engel emphasizes that people tend to vary in their ability to experience and cultivate it. It's more something you *do* than something you merely feel by accident. Happy people tend to have a very particular way of looking at life, including setbacks and adversity, and possess an optimistic and hopeful disposition that actively seeks the upside in all situations.

A low happiness factor is often a major predictor of discord in relationships of all kinds, and is an especially useful thing to learn to detect in others. Clues to a person's happiness trait include noticing how resilient they are. **Pay attention to how they explain their own flaws and weaknesses to themselves, as well as how they interpret misfortune** in their own or others' lives. The lens they place on neutral events will tell you a lot about the way they think.

Sociability

How much capacity does this person have for friendship and camaraderie? Are they able to be loyal, friendly, and tolerant?

Clues to sociability are to be found in the person's social connections (we will explore this more in a later chapter). The number of friends is not important, but their quality is. Be curious about why a person may have no friends, and pay attention to how they talk about their friends—especially the ones they have conflicts with.

Do they ask about other people and remember them? Do they know how to make others feel welcome and are they patient and enduring when it comes to people's foibles? **Look at the kinds of friendships the person has and consider what they're based on**—convenience, similarity, or something else?

Capacity for Intimacy

Finally, an important trait to consider, especially if you're interested in someone romantically. If two people are badly mismatched in their capacity for intimacy, then of course there will be misunderstandings and conflict. Perhaps of all the traits, this one is worth actually observing rather than making assumptions based on cultural expectations.

How able is someone to trust, to be vulnerable, to receive and give love, to commit, to communicate, and to regulate their own emotions? A person's emotional and relational intelligence can easily be read when you consider that every conversation or interaction is a reflection of that person's overall relational temperament.

In other words, the way they approach the conversation will reveal broader patterns with others. An easy way to plumb for this kind of information is to **ask people harmless questions about their childhoods, and note the way they talk about it**. Yet again, the content doesn't matter—but their emotional intelligence in relaying that content does.

Notice if people seem cold or aloof, or if they tend to shy away from giving or receiving care. As a "test," you could playfully reveal a tiny "secret" and watch their response. A person with a high capacity for intimacy will recognize this bid for closeness and respond warmly with a mini secret of their own. A person with a low capacity might not register your little invitation, or may outright rebuff it.

Goodness

Most people in the modern world are unaccustomed to thinking about life in moral terms. One's ability to do the just thing, to be good, to know right from wrong, and to take ethical action, however, is a character trait that is hard to overestimate—for obvious reasons, you wouldn't want to get too heavily involved with a person who has a weak sense of morality!

Clues to a person's moral character are abundant, if one cares to look. **Notice how empathetic a person is, especially when there is no clear benefit to them in caring for someone else.** Be very curious if they're highly skilled at justifying morally dubious behavior—for example, you catch them lying comfortably to others, gossiping, cheating, or otherwise being deceitful. Again, it's not the acts themselves you are watching for, but rather how the person explains and justifies them that will give you a peek into their "goodness."

In fact, goodness is such a useful and interesting trait to observe that we will dedicate our next chapter to it.

The Server Test

You may have already heard the advice to watch how people treat servers, since this will tell you a lot about their character and moral fiber. In fact, many CEOs and business leaders still take clients to expensive lunches not so they can discuss the matters at hand, but rather so that they can observe the *people* at hand.

The idea is simple. **The way you treat a person when there are no real social consequences either way is a great indicator of overall "goodness," kindness, and consideration.** In a business setting, people may well be gracious and attentive, but it's difficult to know whether they are faking this for strategic reasons. How people treat waitstaff, however, shows you their true baseline—this is how they think of people they *don't* stand to gain anything from. If you're a shrewd businessman, you know that observing this behavior gives you a good indicator of how a person might behave when things aren't going their way, or when they perceive that you are no longer useful to them.

In the same way, the server test is great for dating situations since it clearly reveals the person's attitude to those they are not attracted to or trying to impress. A man, for example, may be enormously flattering and attentive to the pretty young woman he is trying to woo, but she'd be wise to notice how he treats the women he isn't attracted to, and who, as servers, are obliged to give him what he wants.

In both work and dating contexts, there is also the question of how a person treats those they see as subordinate to them—if indeed they even think of waiters and waitresses as subordinate in the first place. An insecure businessman might make a show of treating staff rudely because he thinks it bolsters his own social status, and a woman may think that her date is a nice guy if he's *only* nice to her—perhaps she might even see his rudeness to other women as a positive!

The wonderful thing about the server test is that you can conduct it without anybody being any the wiser. A person may be able to put on a false front with the things they think matter— i.e., impressing you—but they may be relatively unguarded when it comes to how they treat "people who don't matter."

As Charles Bayard Mitchell said, "It is the way one treats his inferiors more than the way he treats his equals which reveals one's real character." To that we can add that how one treats one's *superiors* is especially not a good indicator of character! Here are a few more tips for using the server test in your own observations:

Look for the Most Consistent Behavior

As usual, any behavior in isolation doesn't tell you much, but you can start to draw conclusions if you see patterns across many different situations and places. These tend to point to more stable traits. Notice in particular the stability and variability of the trait itself. Does the person tend to behave the same way to others, no matter what? Or do they tend to swing wildly from one to the other? If the latter, it may suggest that this person has a more situational approach, and their empathy and respect for others may be more conditional.

Watch Their Response to Mistakes

Some people may be all sweetness and light—until the waiter messes up their order, that is. Watch very closely. You're about to see how a person handles conflict, how they deal with disappointment, how assertive they are, and their communication style in general. Not only will you witness their level of empathy, but you can also pick up on other details—do they make things personal? Can they laugh off mistakes? Do they go out of their way to be patient and understanding, or do they almost seem to enjoy being offended? You are getting a little glimpse into how it might be to fall into conflict with this person yourself!

Notice Their Confidence Levels

The server test is not just for determining whether people are nice or not. It can reveal a lot more about people, in particular how assertive, calm, and confident they are. Have you noticed how some people would rather die than politely ask for salt or alert the staff their order is wrong? Others have no qualms about speaking up and do so respectfully and with a feeling of conviction that they'll ultimately get what they want.

Pay attention to how people engage with waitstaff in general and you will see their entire attitude come to life. Some people may feel, for example, that they have to be a little mean to have their needs met (a sign of low self-esteem), while others take a very neutral, almost detached approach that takes emotion out of it completely. Notice if people are flirting with waitstaff, hogging their attention, getting awkward around them, or treating them as though they're simply invisible. In context, what does each of these behaviors suggest to you?

Summary:

- There are many clues and hints that a person is ready to end a conversation; look closely, as most people will downplay these signals out of politeness. Look for verbal, nonverbal, and other clues such as concluding/departing statements and gestures, standing, packing up, and so on. Realize that most casual conversations tend not to last longer than ten minutes.
- Not all interruptions are created the same—know the difference between competitive overlapping (trying to wrest attention away from the speaker, flow stopped) and cooperative overlapping (maintaining attention on the speaker, flow not stopped). The difference is the function and intention of the interruption. Notice how people interrupt one another (given context), and you can learn a lot about their relationships, communication styles, and power dynamics.
- When it comes to judging character, there are six domains you could observe:

intelligence, drive, sociability, capacity for intimacy, happiness, and goodness.
- Pay attention to how (not what) a person thinks, what their goals are and how they respond to obstacles to those goals, how they interpret misfortune, and how they talk about and to others—especially when there is no direct benefit to them.
- This last point can be seen in the server test—notice how people treat waiters and waitresses if you want to see their true colors. Notice people's overall confidence levels, their responses to others' mistakes, and their most consistent and repeated behavior.

Chapter 3: Challenge Your Assumptions to Build Real Empathy

What's the biggest impediment to properly reading and understanding other people?

The answer is *not* other people's complexity, contradictions, secrecy, ambiguity, or complex personalities. In fact, it's got nothing to do with the people we are trying to read at all. **Rather, the biggest threat to our ability to read others well lies in us.** Our own assumptions, judgments, biases, unrealistic expectations, and unexamined beliefs may get in the way of us properly seeing and understanding the people in front of us. They almost certainly can be a roadblock to genuine empathy.

In this chapter, let's explore some ways to remove these roadblocks so that we can learn to cultivate real insight, empathy, and understanding for other people.

The Illusion of Asymmetric Insight

In the previous section, we looked at how to interpret people's behavior toward servers. While it's easy to conclude that someone who is rude to servers is probably rude in general, it's harder when dealing with more ambiguous behavior. For example, what does it mean if someone orders a salad versus a steak? How can you interpret their wanting to pay, deciding to have the cheapest/most expensive meal, fidgeting with the saltshakers, or avoiding eye contact with the people at the next table?

Speaking plainly, **when we are dealing with ambiguous stimuli, there is always a chance that we introduce error simply by the fact of our own biases**. We see someone order a salad and project onto them our own opinions about what a salad means; we conclude that they must be on a diet, that they must not like how they look, that they must be punishing themselves and have low self-esteem . . . yet chances are if *you* ordered a salad at a restaurant, you would protest all these heavy interpretations, right? "I ordered a salad because I felt like eating a salad!"

It turns out there is a name for this kind of cognitive distortion: It's called the illusion of asymmetric insight, and it's exactly what it sounds like. To explain the bias, try it yourself right now. Look at the following missing-letter words and complete them with the first thing that comes to mind:

CH _ _ T

B _ _ K

S _ _ RE

G _ _ L

STR _ _ _

SL _ T

Now the question is, do you think that the way you completed these words tells you something deep and meaningful about who you are as a person? Chances are, no.

In fact, this is the format of a real research experiment, which found that most people readily denied that this test revealed anything special about them. How could it, right? It's just a few words. The funny thing is that people tended to assume that *other people's responses* to such a word test did in fact reveal important things about them. They were very ready to speculate on what those meanings were, to assign values and interpretations, and to spot all sorts of complex patterns.

While we would find such characterizations unfair when applied to us, they seem natural when we make them about others. The illusion of asymmetric insight, then, has a few components. It is the belief that:

- Other people's behavior and choices is somehow more revealing than our own.
- We know and understand others more than they know and understand us.
- We know ourselves more deeply than other people know themselves.

In other words, we believe that our own perception of others is somehow richer and more complex, and that we can see into other people's worlds in a way that we don't seem to imagine is reciprocated. It's understandable why we have this bias. Because we are always in our own heads, it's easy to believe that our own inner worlds are so much more complex than other people's, and it's easier to imagine that *we* can conceal our depths, but that others are transparent and straightforward. Most of us tend to think that other people are what they appear to be, while we ourselves are a little more complicated and that who we really are is not all that accessible to others.

If we routinely overestimate our own complexity and readability while underestimating everyone else's . . . we're going to be bad at reading social dynamics. This is because we will fail to really consider situational influences and be too ready to inject our own assumptions into a situation and read things that simply aren't there. Sometimes, people appoint themselves as good judges of character, but all whilst they have never actually confirmed their predictions. They see someone, make a conjecture about who they are, and then congratulate themselves for being so astute. Meanwhile the person in question is never consulted! There is, in other words, a fine line between *reading* people and blindly *judging* them.

Stereotypes and lazy assumptions are bad for obvious reasons, but they also damage your ability to accurately observe social dynamics. **We need to constantly guard against the human tendency to be overly confident in our own opinions, perceptions, and thoughts.**

When people first begin to improve their social skills and learn to read social dynamics, they may temporarily enjoy creating quite limited and unflattering profiles of others. If this sounds familiar, gently remind yourself how annoying it is to be on the receiving end of an overly simplistic and completely inaccurate personality judgment from someone who actually hasn't taken the time to truly watch and listen.

Always be willing to ask if you are really seeing a person or are just seeing what you want to see. Have you learned something about them, or have you just convinced yourself that your knee-jerk assumption seems true?

The great thing is that knowledge really is power. Now that you know this illusion exists and is fairly common, you can be alert to it and take steps to counteract it. One interesting possibility, however, is to use this very bias as a source of information in itself.

For example, let's go back to our word completion task at the beginning. If someone read the last word and completed it as "SLUT," it probably doesn't mean anything. Yet, someone else might observe this and make a whole bunch of conjectures: "This person seems judgmental. They're clearly insecure about sexuality. If they're female, I bet they have some internalized shame or something. If male, maybe this guy is a little bit old-fashioned?"

Completing the word that way means nothing, but it certainly means something that the observer made the interpretations they did! By what they claim to see in other people, you can probably infer more about *them* than you can the first person.

We've already seen that observing people's friendships and how they talk about others can yield interesting information, and this bias helps us understand why. Other people are like Rorschach blots, and you can learn a lot about someone by the way they describe, explain, interpret, and attribute the behavior of other people. We will explore this concept in more depth in a later chapter, but for now let's look at more concrete ways to make sure that this bias is not interfering with our own ability to read social dynamics properly.

Avoid Hasty Judgments

The truth is that we can listen, observe, ask questions, and pay close attention all *without* judging. We do not need to rush in and make a pronouncement (in fact, we don't need to make a pronouncement at any time) or explain everything or find a convenient label for someone. Think of it this way: The moment you have convinced yourself that you have someone all figured out is the moment you stop gathering information about them.

Instead, just stay in the moment without trying to rush to any conclusion. Notice everything but be slow to make any final declarations. Finally, be patient. Nobody can peek into your deepest soul just by watching you for a few minutes, right? The same is true for other people!

Challenge Your Own Assumptions

The only way you can challenge your assumptions, of course, is to be aware that you even have them in the first place. Question your assumptions about others' experiences and perspectives. You will probably have a knee-jerk response to them, but don't settle on this without questioning it a little further.

Keep in mind what's called the Johari window, which explains that every person is comprised of:
- The Open Area (known to yourself, and known to others too)
- The Blind Spot (unknown to yourself, but known to others)
- The Hidden Area (known to yourself, but unknown to others)
- The Unknown (unknown to yourself, and unknown to others too)

You *may* be able to see into someone else's blind spot or their hidden area, but don't assume it. You might see a behavior—let's say, keeping very quiet in meetings—and believe you are seeing material in their blind spot (i.e., that they are reserved, unconfident) when really what you are seeing is plainly in the open area and doesn't quite mean what you think it does. In this case, the person may not be reserved at all, but simply respectful or disinterested or so confident in themselves they don't *need* to speak. You get the idea.

Bear in mind also that there will be a big part of people that you simply can never see— including those parts that they themselves don't even know about. As long as you can have a basic respect for the complexity and depth of others, you will only be a better social reader and judge of character, not a worse one.

Keep gathering data. One effective way to overcome the illusion of asymmetric insight is to not assume, but to do the work of gathering more real information. That means listening well, observing, asking direct questions, and paying very close attention to what the responses are.

One enormous but underappreciated way to gather good quality information is to seek feedback about your interpretations and judgments. Of course, this won't always be appropriate, but there's no rule that you have to be a sneaky detective in the shadows. If you're curious, run your appraisals by the person in question: "You seem like someone who really values family . . . Have I got that right?"

The funny thing is that people will often bend themselves out of shape trying to guess and conjecture when others would be perfectly happy to tell them everything they wanted to know if they'd only ask!

Reflect on times you've gotten things wrong—they are great opportunities for you to learn something and do better next time. If you often find yourself being surprised to learn something new about someone, it may be time to reflect and see whether your assumptions about them were too narrow.

Susan Fiske's Stereotype Content Model

If it's true that we tend to assume we have more insight into others than we really do, then we need to ask where all this "insight" is coming from, if not the person who is actually in front of us. **Chances are, we are relying on stereotypes, which are nothing more than crystallized cultural assumptions and expected social patterns.** If we don't really know who someone is, it makes sense that the next best thing is to observe what we can and fill in the blanks with whatever stereotype looks like it fits best.

Using stereotypes is not necessarily a sign of being a prejudiced person or having poor social skills—quite the opposite. Stereotypes evolved naturally because throughout our human history, we have had to make quick judgments about people based on very little. Stereotypes are not harmful because they're *always* untrue and insulting—they're harmful precisely because they happen to be true some of the time!

In order to become more adept at reading social dynamics as they really are (versus just lazily resorting to guesswork), it's a good idea to actually try to understand what stereotypes are and how they function. This is where the stereotype content model (SCM) comes in handy.

The SCM is a theory explaining how stereotypes can be characterized as a function of two variables: warmth and competence. We can imagine the matrix created by these two variables as follows (image adapted from toolshero):

	Competence	
	High	Low
Warmth High / warm	Admiration	Pity
Low / cold	Envy	Contempt

Depending on the combination of these two variables, we see stereotypes grouped into clusters. The model was originally developed by Susan Fiske and colleagues in 2002, who was curious about the fact that not all stereotypes were the same. In addition, she found that stereotypes of incompetence, for example, tended to come with stereotypes of warmth. This kind of stereotype (low competence, high warmth) is common in the way we speak of elderly people, or other ethnicities that we feel are inferior but mostly harmless.

The model has been shown to hold across cultures and has been in use in social psychology since its creation. Let's take a closer look at the two dimensions:

Warmth in this context means (perceived) trustworthiness, friendliness, and likeability. It is the feeling we get from people we assume are good and nice, who are able to socially harmonize with others and pose no threat. They are easy to empathize with and seen as honest and broadly reliable.

Competence is about action and the (perceived) degree to which someone is able to carry out a particular task. Capability is more respected than liked, but it conveys intelligence, skill, intentionality, power, and sometimes independence.

Combining these two, we get:

High Warmth + High Competence = Admiration

When someone is both capable *and* nice to be around, we admire them. People who are judged according to these stereotypes are seen as natural and rightful leaders.

Low Warmth + High Competence = Envy

People who are just as capable but who do not demonstrate warmth and likeability may earn stereotypes that are begrudgingly respectful but also include jealousy. There is sometimes a feeling of the competence being unearned (since the person is perceived to be "bad" and therefore not deserving of their skill), and this results in envy.

High Warmth + Low Competence = Pity

When people are judged to be broadly incapable but generally good and nice, the resulting stereotypes hinge around pity. Their perceived inferiority is softened by the fact that they are likeable; many people consider warmth overall more valuable and so will regard a nice but incompetent person with far more tolerance than a capable but cold person.

Low Warmth + Low Competence = Contempt

The worst of both worlds, these stereotypes are about people who are perceived as doubly inferior—they are not only useless, but also bad, which implies that they are somehow choosing or amplifying their own uselessness. This combination leads to a feeling that such people deserve condemnation.

Broadly speaking, incompetent people are tolerated if they're also warm, and are considered more likeable than equally competent people who are cold. It's best to be seen as both warm and competent; those perceived to have neither are considered fair game for disapproval and social exclusion.

As you read through the above descriptions, you might have thought of a few common stereotypes that fit the description. The great thing about this model is that it encompasses all types of stereotypes, including the "positive" ones. Many people argue that there's no harm in holding certain stereotypes (women are sweet and nice but not as smart, disabled children are incompetent but kind of cute in a patronizing way, etc.) yet Fiske's model shows us that these assumptions are prejudices all the same. In fact, feeling a kind of superior condescension toward someone may be felt to be *more* insulting than merely envying them for their talents.

Now, it's important to remind ourselves at this point that Fiske's model is *not* a personality model—she is not outlining the different kinds of people that exist in the world. Rather, she is laying out a model of common ways that we *perceive* others. Our job is not to correctly identify others according to where they fall on these two parameters (that's a different book entirely!) but rather to start understanding and categorizing our own perceptions.

How to Use Fiske's model

We can use the SCM to improve our understanding of social dynamics and become better judges of individual character. Though it may be true that you can read people as either more warm or cold, and as more competent or incompetent, the really interesting insights come from exploring the ways that these concepts themselves are used as a form of communication.

1. Think about people's intentions

What we perceive when we observe others is a blend of who they really are (naturally and spontaneously) and who they are consciously choosing to project themselves as. It's a little like the difference between a natural smile and a "fake" one discussed earlier. We all use stereotypes when we observe others, but of course, people can employ stereotypes *in the way they present themselves.*

Pay close attention to how people are showing up socially in terms of these two dimensions. Notice the choices they are making and think about what this might mean about who they are and what they are trying to communicate. For example, you may observe an extremely competent woman deliberately playing down her ability when with male colleagues. Think about why she might be doing this and how her use and manipulation of stereotypes might be serving her own ends. Think about the server test again and consider how someone might be deliberately acting cold and aloof while emphasizing their capabilities—are they trying to create envy in others?

2. Think about the stereotypes you buy into

There's no question that we all have assumptions, biases, and preconceived ideas about who people are. Whenever you meet someone new, quickly check in with yourself if you might be making assumptions about them based on some stereotype you hold. Ask how you perceive this person to be in terms of warmth and competence, and see where they fall according to Fiske's model.

The point, of course, is not to profile people and leave it at that; rather, you are making yourself aware of potential bias and even prejudice so that you can constantly check it against reality. Stereotypes are just cognitive shorthand. If you notice you're defaulting to a stereotype, that's okay, but use that as a very *provisional placeholder* and assume that once you get to know the person better, they will naturally appear far more complex than they seemed at first.

3. Think about how others are using stereotypes

You can often gain really good insight into social dynamics—especially conflicts and misunderstandings—by checking to see if stereotypes are playing a role. Stereotypes tend to lead to predictable patterns of behavior toward the person being stereotyped.

Warm and competent groups are admired and respected. They are listened to, afforded privileges, trusted, believed, and given the benefit of the doubt.

Cold and incompetent groups are viewed negatively and often dismissed. They may earn active scorn, criticism, judgment, or ostracism.

Cold but competent groups may evoke jealousy or resentment. Ironically, people may work hard to tear such people down, explain away their competence, or focus on judging them for their coldness, while ignoring their competence.

Warm but incompetent groups may receive sympathetic or patronizing treatment. They may be let off the hook (held to lower standards), be overlooked, or have others speak for them (this has important ramifications for the social phenomenon of tantrums, which we will discuss later).

Working backward, if you notice some of these behaviors in a social dynamic, you can ask if they are the result of how someone is being perceived. For example, you may observe interactions within a big family and notice that the grandmother is loved and cherished but largely ignored and denied the status of a competent adult and treated almost as one of the children. Or you might notice that a couple is arguing, and seeing how they talk to one another, you realize that they have both started to perceive each other as low on both warmth and competence (hence, contempt is running rife).

4. Think about how you come across

Although this book is about improving your understanding of social dynamics in others, it certainly doesn't hurt to spare a thought for the stereotypes others might be tempted to apply to you, and adjust accordingly. Some people, for example, worry that they are not popular and so in vain work very hard to be more competent, then are confused when this does not automatically lead to people liking them. Others may be confused about why they are earning envy and distrust when they simply want to be liked and accepted, and others can't shake the feeling that they are liked but somehow not respected or taken seriously.

Think about the signals you send, the stereotypes you conform to, and what you can do to actively send the message you want to send to others.

Becoming a Tuning Fork

Earlier, we mentioned how much can be learned from becoming aware of *your own* facial expressions and the modulations in your own voice in order to gain insight into what might be happening with *the other person*. **Humans naturally mimic and mirror one another, even unconsciously, such that when you read yourself, you are also reading your reaction to others around you, which is in effect the same as reading them.**

This has been called the chameleon effect (Chartrand and Bargh 1999) and will not come as a surprise to anyone who has closely observed social interactions, including those that happen between very young infants and their mothers. In fact, this kind of bodily mirroring of others can be understood as the more primal foundation of what we know as empathy—when we say "I know how you feel," there may be more truth in this than we realize.

This mimicry and reflection don't just happen in real time, either. Have you ever noticed how you eventually start to mimic certain expressions, turns of phrase, gestures, and little quirks that originally belonged to a friend or partner? This is something that happens all on its own—trying things out in our own voice, and with our own bodies, is a path into other people's experiences.

It's what allows us to empathize, and when we consciously mirror others, it can build and create empathy in more deliberate ways. Researchers have found that those who measure high on empathy tend to show high levels of mimic behavior (Chartrand and Bargh 1999), but the relationship goes the other way, too: When we want to demonstrate our empathy and understanding to others, we can choose to deliberately mirror others.

For example, if you meet someone abroad who hails from your hometown, you may either automatically or deliberately choose to emphasize your hometown accent so it more closely matches theirs. It's as though you are literally saying, "I understand! I speak the same language as you!" We can mirror someone's happy grin as they tell us exciting news, we can match the pace, tone, and pitch of their speech as they relay a painful episode, or we can pick up on unique word choices or metaphors and repeat them back, showing in a subtle but powerful way that we have really heard and absorbed their message.

Throughout this book, we've been practicing, in one way or another, how to make the unconscious more conscious. We are all unconsciously broadcasting reams of data about ourselves in social situations, but this information flies underneath the radar of conscious awareness. **Social geniuses and people-readers have learned to notice the unnoticed and put it to good use.**

So, how can you make use of the existence of the chameleon effect and the fact that people unconsciously mirror one another?

Intelligence officers and professional interrogators often explain a little-known aspect of their work: When watching interviews or interactions from afar, they often put their attention not on the person in question, but on the person interviewing them. By watching the reaction of the interviewer to the interviewee, they glean all sorts of information—it's as though the interviewer becomes an unconscious tuning fork, picking up on and exhibiting all sorts of hidden currents and energies.

How can this be? Well, you can try a little experiment right now. Find a picture of a person showing a pronounced facial expression—despair or joy or surprise—and look at the picture for a little while. Now, after a while, you might notice something interesting: Your own face might be ever so slightly altered. That's because, in your attempt to read and understand what the people in front of you are feeling, your own face has made tiny contractions to mirror what it's seeing. This is like a muscular kind of empathy.

The funny thing is, you might feel like you don't know what the person in the picture is feeling, but if you quickly pay attention to what your own features are doing, it suddenly becomes clear. Have you ever had a "feeling" about someone? It may be because your body knew something you didn't!

The James–Lange theory of emotion is the idea that, for example, we don't smile because we feel happy, but rather we feel happy because we notice we are smiling. To extend this, we don't know if someone else is feeling happy unless we match their expression with our own face and feel a tiny bit of that happiness ourselves. Thinking now about the chameleon effect, we can see social mirroring as a kind of active and automatic attempt to understand people.

So why not use this effect deliberately?

If you are trying to get a better read on the people around you, don't forget to consult yourself as a finely tuned, sophisticated social instrument! Check in with what "reading" you are getting. Since this often happens beneath the level of conscious awareness, you may be surprised at what you find out when you stop to check in with yourself this way. While much of what we focus on in this book enlists the help of our conscious cognitive power, the truth is that our body itself is a powerful tool of perception—an unconscious one.

Skillful therapists can take years to develop what is sometimes called "embodied countertransference" (Stone 2006). This is where the therapist learns to read and interpret their own bodily responses to their clients and mine them as a source of data about what is going on with that client. Naturally, such a task is fraught with complications!

Nevertheless, anyone can learn to become a better "human tuning fork," and one way to do this is to start with an accurate baseline reading:

- Become aware. Stop for a second and take a few deep breaths.
- Now, imagine that your awareness is like a beam of light shining in turn over every area of your body, or a "scanner" beam passing over your body from top to toe. What do you notice? What sensations stand out to you?
- Try to memorize this particular body state as your personal neutral.

Now that you know what neutral feels like, you can assume that any variations from this state are a result of being engaged in a particular social interaction. Let's say you go on a first date, and as the date unfolds, you chat about this and that, have some coffee, and then agree to meet later in the week. As you say goodbye, you immediately pause again and take another reading—how do you feel *now* compared to your initial baseline?

Perhaps you notice, for the first time, that there is actually quite a lot of tension all across your neck and shoulders. You notice that there is a rather weird and unpleasant feeling in the pit of your stomach. You realize you've been holding your breath. Now, you can recognize the fact that first dates are usually nerve-wracking and that the caffeine in the coffee might be playing a role (here are our four Cs again!), but once you pay attention to these sensations, you realize that there was something not right about the interaction. You notice you feel uneasy and a little on guard.

Now, you would not have noticed any of this had you only paid attention to what your date told you verbally, or if you noticed only their nonverbal behavior and not your own. Somehow, during the date, your body was responding to the situation with microscopic contractions that reflected something important in the situation.

Naturally, we don't want to get into the habit of blaming others or assuming that *everything* we feel must be somehow related to other people. It's essential to get a baseline reading and to not make any hasty conclusions based on small amounts of data. For example, you may go on a second date to confirm your first impressions, rather than immediately conclude that the person wasn't right for you.

A great way to think of it is to see your body as just another useful and valid data point in the bigger picture—one of many sources of information. When you're making observations and interpretations, always remember that you yourself are usually an integral part of a social situation. If you are a part of the dynamic, reading yourself gives you access to understanding a part of that dynamic!

It's especially useful when your body is sending you conflicting information. Discrepancies and mismatches can point to misunderstandings or, more commonly, concealment, manipulation, or deception. For example, the person in front of you may be smiling warmly and saying all the right things, but there's a part of you that is registering that their smile is not sincere. Notice that you feel "off" about this person. Notice how you are telling yourself, "I don't like him, but I don't really have a reason." You *do* have a reason—become curious about what it might be.

Sometimes people feel absolutely drained after socializing with certain individuals or groups, and blame themselves for it since the people in question appear to be friendly and nice. On closer inspection, your fatigue after every interaction is telling you something important about the real dynamics that lurk beneath—these people may be unconsciously siphoning off enormous amounts of energy from you, or you may be unconsciously picking up on how exhausted *they* are despite appearances.

Finally, when you're reading other people, remember to also read others as they are interacting with them. Let's say you're watching a friend group. There is a "clown" character who tends to dominate, always laughing and making jokes, but when you put your attention on those watching him, you can't help but notice the slightly unsettled, anxious expressions on their faces. They just might be reflecting to you some of the more hidden aspects of the clowning behavior you're seeing reflected outwardly.

Developing Empathy to Read People

We've considered at length the many things that can get in the way of us accurately reading others and the social dynamics they inhabit (the illusion of asymmetric insight, stereotypes, or disregarding the data coming from our own bodies). But simply removing these impediments doesn't automatically grant us deep empathy or insight into other people's worlds. In this section, we'll look at practical ways to develop empathy.

Emotionally comprehending and understanding another person's reality as if it were one's own are not some inborn superpowers, but something that any of us can learn to do. Empathy is not difficult, but it is a skill that can become neglected if we don't take the time to nurture and cultivate it. Especially if we're socially anxious, we may simply forget that others exist and that their emotional reality may be very different from our own.

While many books will help you develop your capacity for empathy on moral grounds, and simply because it's a great thing to do for your relationships and your own well-being, for our intents and purposes, empathy is actually a useful skill **because it helps us gather high-quality and actionable data from others**.

This is what allows us to graduate from mere observation and practice to deep understanding and insight into others, beyond the surface level. Emotions are not just some kind of irrelevant icing on the cake of life—rather, they mediate everything else, adding color, meaning, and weight to everything we do as people.

In other words, if we wish to understand how people think, their motivations, their values, their blind spots, their ambitions, their flaws, and their communication styles, we will have to pay close attention to their emotional experience, which influences all these things.

Importantly, empathy also helps us avoid or mitigate the influence of our *own* emotional reality. For example, imagine you observe a small child who is behaving strangely—they are afraid of something that you, as an adult, find totally silly, perhaps even amusing.

You know "the truth"—i.e., that there is nothing to be afraid of—but knowing this and inhabiting your own emotional reality, you are prevented from really seeing into the child's emotional reality, which is one of completely real fear. Mere observation will simply reveal to you a young child afraid of something silly. But *empathetic* observation will allow you to see the entire situation from the child's point of view. Suddenly, you are dealing with a dynamic that is very different! Suddenly, you are empowered to act in a way you would not have been were you merely understanding "the truth" of the situation.

Empathy is not just something nice, merely the way we feel, but *an act of perception*. In the same way as we have to practice being better readers, work hard at learning new skills, and even struggle sometimes in our attempts to learn something valuable, we have to be patient, consistent, and diligent when it comes to learning about what is arguably the most fascinating topic on the face of the earth: the inner worlds of other people.

According to philosopher and cognitive scientist Paul Thagard and psychologist Allison Barnes, empathy can be understood as expressed through several different "modes":

Analogy Mode

In this mode, empathy operates through emotional analogy, a kind of imaginative metaphor. Individuals consciously recognize similarities between their own experiences and perceptions and the observed situation of the other person. So, someone stubs their toe, and you cringe for them, recalling exactly how painful it was for you when you stubbed your toe. Here, you use your own experience as a kind of bridge to grasp and understand another's experience.

Mirroring Mode

We have already explored this aspect of mirroring and reflection—i.e., when we adopt the expressions, language, and body postures of those we engage with, we experience a visceral reaction that tells us something important about how they are feeling. So, you might never have stubbed your toe, but when someone else does, and you see the expression on their face and hear them yelp in pain, the corresponding mirror neurons fire in your own brain and countless tiny changes in your own muscles mirror those of the other person, helping you understand "Ouch, that must *really* hurt!"

Embodied Simulation Mode

This mode of empathy is also nonverbal, but inspired by work covered in Sandra Murray and Richard Holmes's 2011 book, *Interdependent Minds*. They explain how people live by unconscious embodied "rules" that organize their perceptual and emotional realities, and which they can then express verbally. An example of such a rule is: "IF partner demands, THEN resist" or "IF emotion expressed, THEN praise and reward."

Embodied simulation empathy is then about determining what others feel by using your own rules to recreate, or simulate, the other person's reality. For example, you might observe that your partner has the rule "IF partner demands, THEN resist" but are also aware that you yourself have the rule "IF resisting, THEN feel safe." Your empathy here allows you to make the leap and guess that your partner, in resisting your demands, may be doing so in order to feel safe. This is informed guesswork, mediated by your own embodied experience, which results in empathy.

Now, all this might seem rather technical and unfamiliar, but there are many ways to strengthen the empathy skill. The third mode described above in particular can be developed by practicing the perceptual positions technique below. The general idea is to practice becoming aware of many different possible perspectives you can inhabit in any social dynamic, and by doing so, you gain a deeper sense of empathy for other people, but also a richer and more complete view of the entire situation.

Perceptual Positions

The goal here is again to simulate another person's reality in our own minds. We can never literally feel what it's like to be someone else, but we can run a model in our minds, and that model is a good model to the extent that it can help us understand the other person, communicate with them effectively, and predict their behavior. Basically, a mental model of another person's world is good if it helps us make sense of an emotional reality that we are not ourselves experiencing.

This technique comes from NLP (neurolinguistic programming) and helps us build empathy, create more objective perception and self-awareness, and uncover new perceptions previously hidden to us. Done well, the exercise can help us communicate better, resolve conflict more effectively, persuade others, listen well, and show people genuine care.

Here's a simple way to start practicing this technique:

Step 1: Clarify what the situation is

Start by drawing a line around the exact social dynamic or situation you want to understand better. Who is involved, what was said, and what events occurred (or are about to occur)?

Step 2: Practice perspective switching

There are broadly four perceptual positions that you can occupy with your attention and awareness:

The **first** is the default one; your own position, seeing things through your eyes.

The **second** position is where we see the same situation but through someone else's eyes.

The **third** is where we see both ourselves and the other person through the (real or imagined) eyes of a third party, a neutral observer.

There is also the possibility of a **fourth** position, where we in turn observe this observer.

You will immediately improve your empathic abilities simply by realizing that there is more than one way to see things, and that your particular way is just one of many. It takes self-awareness to realize that you are not neutral and objective, but filtering the world through your own mental models and maps of reality, which includes your assumptions, expectations, beliefs, ideas, emotional perceptions, and meanings.

When we switch to perceptual positions other than our own, we try to view the world through their map—and in the fourth position, we do our best to try to guess at the world as it is without being exposed to a particular map at all.

Which position is "right"? Well, none of them. They are all just different viewpoints on the same situation, different lenses. The value of this exercise comes not from identifying the best point of view, but from discovering an enriched and expanded view.

Too many people hold the subtle belief that empathy and perspective switching are nothing more than a little trick to help you understand someone else's weird distortion on reality while assuming that you hold no such distortions. This is why it's so important to embark on this exercise with the right attitude. We have to be patient, curious, and respectful. The name of the game is flexibility.

As you consider these positions in turn, you might like to actually move around from one position in a room or between different rooms to emphasize the real shift in perspective you're trying to achieve. Literally get up and sit in the seat the other person is sitting in, or make an effort to be in the physical, linguistic, and social environment they inhabit.

Take the time in each position to ask yourself questions to gain information on the situation from that point of view:

- How do you explain or make sense of the situation/problem? What do you see?
- Why is it a problem for you?
- What are you thinking and feeling?
- What are you doing and saying? Why?
- What do you value and is that under threat in this situation?
- What are your strengths and insights here?
- What are you trying to achieve? What are your needs here?
- How do you perceive the other person in this situation? What do you think their needs are?
- What do you think *they* are thinking and feeling?

When you shift into the third perspective, become curious about observing the relationship as a whole. What kind of dynamic is playing out? What kind of relationship is this? Try to imagine how you would describe the situation in completely neutral terms, like a journalist or scientist (i.e., no personal investment or emotion—just relaying factual data).

If it seems appropriate, you can also switch to the fourth position and observe the observer, but this may not always be necessary. Try to get a "God's-eye view" of the situation where you synthesize everything from the previous three positions. It's a great idea to then work your way through the positions one more time to see if any additional insight occurs to you. Chances are, by the time you return to your own perspective, things will seem a little different. You will likely also see a new way forward and have more clarity, compassion, and understanding for all involved.

Step 3: Put it all together

Take a few minutes to reflect and write down your insights from each position:

- What did you learn about yourself and your own reactions?
- What insights did you gain about other people's perspectives and motivations?

- How can this understanding guide your next moves? Think not only about how you'll resolve this current situation, but how you might approach other similar situations in the future.

The exercise will become easier and more productive the more you practice it. Take pains to adopt perspectives in good faith—i.e., don't secretly transplant your own perceptions into someone else's mind. Remember that you are not trying to see someone else's world through your eyes, but to see *their* world through *their* eyes—big difference.

For example, you may, from the first position, sincerely feel that another person is being purposefully vindictive and spiteful to you in order to hurt you. But this is your perception. If you switch and genuinely consider how they see you, you may be surprised to learn that they feel as though *you* are the enemy who is trying to hurt them! This technique is powerful but requires patience, open-mindedness, and a lot of emotional maturity.

Summary:
- Our own assumptions, judgments, biases, unrealistic expectations, and unexamined beliefs may get in the way of us properly

understanding and empathizing with people. When dealing with ambiguous stimuli, there is always the chance that we introduce error simply by virtue of our own biases, and we need to guard against this. We need to be alert to the illusion of asymmetric insight in particular, which is in part the belief that we can read others better than they can read us. To be good people-readers, we need to challenge this illusion and question our own judgments.

- Susan Fiske's stereotype content model explains how stereotypes can be characterized as a function of two variables: warmth and competence. Think about how people may be deliberately conforming to stereotypes, or how the stereotypes you hold color your own perception. Notice how stereotypes are deliberately used, rejected, or weaponized by people in social dynamics.
- Humans mimic and mirror one another, such that when you read yourself, you are also reading your reaction to others around you, which is in effect the same as reading them. Your body can become a "tuning fork" that can alert you to other people's emotional realities.
- You can cultivate more empathy by practicing the perceptual positions exercise and deliberately perspective

switching to better empathize with people in a dynamic. By moving through our own position, their position, a neutral third observer, and potentially an observer of the observer, we gain richer insight into social dynamics.

Chapter 4: Understand People by Understanding the Language They Use

Though we have focused so far on reading body language, paralingual signals, and other telltale human behaviors, it's now time to turn to an obvious aspect of social life: words. While nonverbal communication matters, it certainly does not imply that verbal communication doesn't.

The way people use language tells you about the way they tell stories and the way they try to engage others, and gives a clue to the way they may even speak to *themselves* internally. Language, then, is an enormous part of both people's inner worlds and in social dynamics more generally.

We'll examine the connection between what people say and what people *hear*, what it means when people go out of their way to be vague or unclear, and how even casual or seemingly unimportant chitchat can actually reveal people's deep feelings, desires, and fears.

The "Four Ears" Model

You're watching a newly married couple. One of them says, "Oh no, not again, the tank's empty," and the other snaps, "I haven't even driven the car in weeks!"

There is so, so much more beyond the actual words they're communicating, right? The "meta communication" is not in the least about cars or gas. When one commented that the tank was empty, the other "heard" a far larger, more complex message.

Friedemann Schulz von Thun was a German professor who introduced what he called the "four ears" model, and it has a lot in common with the perceptual positions concept discussed earlier. According to Thun, every message a person communicates:

The Fact Layer

What it sounds like: objective and verifiable factual information. In this case, it's a plain fact that the tank is empty.

The Self-Revelation Layer

When we speak, we cannot help but share something of ourselves or our intentions, whether we are aware of it or not, whether we intend it or not. The revelation of ourselves may be obvious, or it may be hidden. For example, saying "the tank's empty" could reveal plenty about the speaker's mindset and focus.

The Relationship Layer

Messages also reveal something about the speaker's beliefs and feelings about the relationship in which they share that information. Observing out loud that the tank is empty may communicate the speaker's feelings about the relationship: "I'm sharing this with you because this is our car, and I see you as interested in the things that concern us both." It might reveal "I'm frustrated."

The Appeal Layer

People communicate for a reason (even if they're not entirely sure what that is). Often, the reason is to appeal for something. For example, "Please share my annoyance with the empty tank. I want empathy and validation." The appeal may also be, "This is a problem. I want you to do something about it."

As you can clearly see, there are many ways to "hear" the same message. Misunderstandings and conflicts occur when people hear things that weren't intended. For example, "Why are you defensive? I wasn't saying that *you* used up the gas and didn't refill the car. I was just saying!"

The same verbal message can come across very differently depending on the nature of the relationship of the speakers, the context, and the history of that ongoing interaction. These background details make the difference between an innocent observation and one person feeling blamed and attacked.

As a neutral observer, you can learn a lot about social interactions by listening not just to the verbal message being shared, but to all the other layers of meaning that accompany it. From this simple exchange, you can note that there are some underlying resentments, perhaps patterns of accusation or unresolved tensions. Reading between the lines in this way is a powerful method for learning to listen for what people are really communicating when they talk to one another.

Now, from a personal point of view, it's great to keep the four ears model in mind when you communicate. It's really important to share your own messages clearly so you are leaving no room for misinterpretation. At the same time, the four ears model allows you to understand why you may not have been heard properly, and what to do about it.

Let's say that you are the person who noticed the empty tank, and then noticed the defensive response. One possibility is that you "hear" blame and accusation in this reaction. You hear, "You're a nasty and rude person and you've upset me and it's unfair." Of course, your reaction to hearing *this* will likely be to become defensive yourself! You can easily see how misunderstandings build on one another and lead to outright conflicts.

Instead, you can choose to listen for the emotional content of what is being communicated and let go of the ego's need to be right. You could smile and quickly clarify. "Oh, oops, I only meant that I see that it's empty and that I need to fill it up. I wasn't saying that you were to blame for anything."

Of course, context matters here, and if you routinely have this sort of misunderstanding with someone, you can start to ask broader questions of what you both believe about the relationship, about the other person, and about what you are primarily trying to share with one another (you will recognize this as the embodied simulation mode of empathy from Murray and Holmes's work described above).

By paying attention to the unspoken rules, assumptions, expectations, and emotional content beneath messages, you become a more artful and empathetic communicator. Clear communication is an act of kindness and compassion. We learn to listen in an expanded way. The sender and receiver are different human beings, living in different worlds of meaning. Real communication is not a question of saying the right thing, winning, or arguing your case persuasively. It's about learning to both observe and use language as a tool for helping you connect with people in a genuine way.

There's far more to the four ears theory than we can cover here in this short chapter, but the big message is that verbal communication doesn't stand alone—the speaker's intentions and the receiver's ability to hear those intentions matter just as much, if not more than, the factual verbal information being shared.

To improve your own communication skills, pay close attention to your own and others' messages and be aware of the layers of meaning both in what is said and what is heard. Remember that you can always check in and confirm with someone—no guesswork required! When communication breaks down or there are misunderstandings, stop and immediately consider how there is likely a mismatch between what is being sent and what is being received.

On the other hand, this model is also useful if you want to become a better judge of character, observer of human behavior, and expert at human social dynamics. Learn to prick your ears for hidden, unspoken information. Learn to notice that fifty percent of a message is what is said ... but fifty percent of it is in how it's received and interpreted. Notice how people respond to one another, and you will instantly be privy to details about their own self-concept, their expectations of the relationship, and their feelings about the situation at hand.

Combined with the skills you are already learning about body language, reading the voice, looking for character clues, and reading the room using the four Cs, you will soon demonstrate powers of observation that start to look like mind-reading!

As you watch, ask yourself the following:

- What is the sender's intention?
- What else might they be implying by their message?
- With what "ear" is the listener listening?
- Does the sending and the receiving align?
- What is the overall reaction and outcome of the message? What effect does it have?
- What does their response tell you about the relationship and their feelings about the sender?
- What does the exchange tell you about the people in question?
- Ultimately, what is the conversation *about*, on all levels?

If you watched the couple having a minor argument about gas in the tank of the car, you might observe that there were really several conversations at once, one about the practical fact of the tank being empty, one about old patterns of blame and resentment, one about the burden of demand and expectation, even some very old conversations that each party brought with them from previous relationships—i.e., the relative role of men and women in marriages, the way to resolve conflict, learned behaviors around how to get others to cooperate with you . . .

That's a lot of information! But it really is there for the taking if you only pay attention. Keep paying attention and each new observation will help you build a nuanced and comprehensive picture not just of the people in front of you but of the complex relational webs that exist between them.

To practice using this model yourself, consider an example and how you would observe and interpret it:

You are walking with a group of friends. Friend A is carrying some takeout coffee cups for the group, and as they approach a closed door, they make a show of visibly struggling to get the door open while their hands are full. They narrow their eyes and frown a little, but still smiling faintly, they say, "Thank you for rushing to help me out here!" Friend B flashes a big grin and says, "Oh, you're welcome!" while pointedly not opening the door. Friend A laughs and says, "What a jerk. I'm not giving you your coffee now," as they awkwardly open the door with their elbow before going inside. Friend B laughs also, saying, "I love you too, Friend A."

Now, asking the questions we listed above and factoring in the various context clues and body language, what can you tell about Friend A and B and, importantly, what can you tell about the relationship *between* them?

Detecting Weasel Words

By now, you're probably getting the strong impression that the actual dictionary definition of words is the least interesting thing about them, and a person's message encompasses far, far more than what they share in a literal sense. People are not robots, and communication is not just about the transfer of data. Consequently, you can learn a lot about people by noticing all the ways they *don't* communicate in perfectly logical, clear ways.

If your goal is to learn to be a better communicator, then the way is obvious: Be clearer and more intentional in the way you express yourself.

If, as with this book, your aim is to learn to become a better reader of people, however, then a lack of clarity becomes an interesting thing, since it reveals so much about the person in question. In other words, **a lack of clarity in one's message is itself a message** and is an aspect of meta-communication that itself can be read.

Enter the concept of "weasel words," which is a term originally coined by Chaplin in 1900 and later popularized by Theodore Roosevelt (who no doubt needed to express what he frequently encountered in political discourse). Weasel words are words that allow people to "weasel out" of the message they really want to send. They consciously or unconsciously dilute the real meaning of words and obscure their implication; the result is language that makes things less certain and clear, rather than the reverse.

Let's say you're a devious politician who wants to conceal the fact that you don't have any hard evidence for your claim, so you preface that claim with "as we all know" or "obviously." He wants to create the feeling of validity without strictly being held to any standards of proof. Similarly, when a parent says, "Maybe, I'll think about it," to a request, they have answered in a way that is really not an answer at all.

Weasel words can be about sugarcoating or softening the blow of unpleasant news, about ever-so-slightly fudging the truth, and also about outright deception and gaslighting, Frequently, new words enter the public consciousness precisely because those in power would like to conceal their real intention or pass one thing off as another. Thus, we see prisons called "correctional" facilities, and propaganda called "education," and we have been taught that any statement following "science says" cannot be challenged. Weasel words really point to an entire spirit of communication that is, well, weaselly.

Sneaky, evasive, and obfuscating language rightly has a bad reputation, but of course there are times and places where euphemistic language and "hedging" language actually are more appropriate. Saying something without saying it requires an enormous amount of empathy, social sophistication, and careful tact and is not to be sniffed at. When the doctor says, "It's *possible*," when a hopelessly terminal cancer patient asks if they could be spontaneously healed, they are being deceptive, but for compassionate reasons.

Being intentionally vague, misleading, or ambiguous is just one way to use language, and for the purposes of this book, we will not be focusing on whether or not to use weasel words in our own communication. Rather, our focus will be on how to observe the use of weasel words in other people so that we can better understand them and the social dynamics they are a part of.

Think of it as a little like taking the third perceptual position, where we become curious about the *function* of weasel words in a relationship rather than merely considering whether they help or harm that particular relationship. Let's take a closer look.

Notice *What* Is Being Obscured or Softened

A person may be reluctant to share their opinions. You may notice them frequently declining to assert their preferences, and when they do, they soften and hedge what they're saying. For example, "Oh, I don't know, maybe we can have pizza? But I don't mind, I guess. I like pizza, I suppose. But we don't have to get pizza, I'm just saying. Maybe. But what do you think? Never mind, I don't know what I want. I'm easy . . ."

Such a person may have low self-esteem or not know how to express their needs directly (watch out—such an inability tends to accompany a genius capacity for manipulation, i.e., the ability to get one's needs met *indirectly*!). They may be avoiding disagreement and confrontation. Consider the other people in the dynamic to explore why this might be.

On the other hand, people may be using weasel words to obscure the facts and details. They say "experts all agree" or "studies show," but don't say what experts or studies. Notice when someone wants to make a claim without being seen to actually make one—i.e., they could technically deny it later in a court of law! You may be witnessing a lack of confidence, a desire not to take responsibility (listen for passive voice—e.g., "mistakes were made"), or an attempt at outright deception. Especially in politics and advertising, weasel words can be used to present a claim as a foregone conclusion. It's a passive, manipulative way of persuading the audience. For example, "We can all agree that XYZ . . ." Really, can we?

To really understand how weasel words function, keep asking what information is being obscured and hidden. If you're having a difficult time getting at the message at all, this is a sign in itself—could the intention actually be to create confusion and lack of clarity?

Notice Wordiness and Unintelligibility

Have you ever noticed that a person who is telling a lie often ends up explaining and justifying themselves far more than an honest person ever would? Have you noticed how some public speakers can seemingly talk for hours but without really saying anything?

Weasel language is often more *voluminous* than clear, direct language. Notice the degree of clarity, the simplicity, the directness, and the sheer volume of what you're being told. For example:

"This, we may add, limited to restrictions imposed by terms of the ordinance, relating to the use of land or the location and character of buildings that may be located thereon, even in the absence of provisions in the contract accepting them, must necessarily be his position for we are convinced, although it must be conceded there are some decisions to the contrary, the rule supported by the better reasoned decisions, indeed if not by the great weight of authority, is that municipal restrictions of such character, existing at the time of the execution of a contract for the sale of real estate, are not such encumbrances or burdens on title as may be availed of by a vendee to avoid his agreement to purchase on the ground they render his title unmerchantable."

What on earth does anything of that mean? Some might argue that its unintelligibility is a big part of the message! Look at it again as a secret, arcane language created exclusively for a select elite to decode and realize that part of the fun may well be to ensure the failure of other parties' comprehension, and you begin to understand the phenomenon of "legalese"!

Notice if people in a social dynamic are deliberately using language that seems designed to make the message harder to discern, not easier. Inappropriate or overly complex language is sometimes used to mystify and impress others, while ambiguity can sometimes be seen for the trick it is: a slight of hand that conceals the fact that the speaker doesn't actually know what they're talking about.

Notice What Is Absent from the Message

The passive voice in particular can hide the main subject of a sentence. For example, "the dog bit the boy" shows that the subject (dog) did an action (bit) to the object (the boy). If you simply say, "The boy was bitten," you are making the subject, the dog, invisible. There are many clever ways to do this, but they invariably tend to point to a deliberate effort to avoid/hide culpability and shift the focus or blame elsewhere. Notice, for example, how some people are swiftly able to shift not just the blame but the entire focus of a conversation:

"You lied to me."

"Look, you're tired. You've been under a lot of stress. Let's talk about this when you're calmer."

There is a lot to be learned by noticing how people change topics or ignore certain tangents. Consider the heaps of information in the following exchange:

"Well, how did the date go? Any chemistry there?"

"He's a really nice guy."

In the above, the juiciest information is not in either utterance, but in the peculiar way one follows from the other: The response is an obvious evasion and not a real answer to the question. These two messages need to be interpreted as a pair. The *relationship* between statement and response is ultimately the most revealing answer of all!

As you pay close attention to the style and manner with which people present themselves, you also have the chance to observe how the message is actually being received by others. Every data point you gather builds a fuller picture. Always remember that language is primarily about sharing information. If the information is distorted, missing, or unintelligible, then prick your ears and try to understand why.

One Big Question

Remember how earlier we said that one big impediment to truly understanding people is letting our own biases and assumptions get in the way? We noted that sometimes we see others not as they truly are but as *we* are. Luckily, we can use knowledge of this fact to our advantage; namely, we can watch the biases and assumptions that emerge in other people as they observe and interpret others. To put it another way, **we can interpret the way that they are interpreting!**

The results of a study titled "Perceiver Effects as Projective Tests: What Your Perceptions of Others Say About You" by Wood, Harms, and Vazire (2010) suggest that we can learn a lot about someone's personality by observing the way they talk about other people's personalities. The way we talk about someone else is a "projective test"—i.e., other people themselves become like Rorschach blots onto which we project our own ideas, assumptions, beliefs, and values.

We have already seen this somewhat at play in the server test, where the way someone treats a server tells you more about them than it does the server in question. The one thing you can ask people that may reveal the most information is, then:

"What do you think of this person?"

Naturally, a person who has a predominantly negative view of other people tends to be quite unhappy or dissatisfied with their own lives, too. And the person who is generous and positive in their descriptions of others tends to likewise be content in their lives and happy with themselves.

According to one of the study's authors, "A huge suite of negative personality traits is associated with viewing others negatively. The simple tendency to see people negatively indicates a greater likelihood of depression and various personality disorders." These perceived traits in others "have consistent relationships with dispositional characteristics of the perceiver, ranging from self-reported personality traits and academic performance to well-being and measures of personality disorders, to how liked the person is by peers."

But it gets far more interesting than this! People tend to see others through a filter or perceptual lens of their own creation. Through this lens, they pick up on certain traits and qualities while ignoring others. What's more, the traits they pick up on are then amplified, interpreted, and explained using that person's own system of meaning. **In other words, the**

thing we use to interpret other people is . . . ourselves.

For example, imagine someone picks up a baby and the baby instantly starts screaming and crying. The person could respond in almost infinite ways. Let's imagine that these are some of their possible responses:

- "Ooh, she doesn't like me!"
- "You poor thing, you miss your mommy, don't you?"
- "That's okay, little guy, I get it. Life's hard, huh?"
- "Wow, haha, babies are so self-centered. Nobody is allowed to have a conversation if they're around."

You've probably heard people make comments just like this. They may seem innocuous (or even accurate!) but the truth is they are mere projections. Babies just cry. Sometimes for no reason. Listening carefully to how someone explains and interprets such a neutral stimulus can tell you where their main point of focus is, what they care about, how they see others (and how they imagine others see them), and the interpretive lenses they place on life.

- **"Ooh, she doesn't like me!"** Here is a person who is telling you they take neutral events personally and have existing mental

models of themselves as unlikeable. This person may be a little self-absorbed or insecure.
- **"You poor thing, you miss your mommy, don't you?"** This person sees distress and interprets it as a longing for human connection. It tells you they may see things in terms of relational connections, have broadly positive models of family life, and expect that other people are a source of soothing and comfort.
- **"That's okay, little guy, I get it. Life's hard, huh?"** This person sees a screaming baby and identifies their own distress with it, imagining that the baby finds life intolerable in the same way they do!
- **"Wow, haha, babies are so self-centered. Nobody is allowed to have a conversation if they're around."** A serious projection. This is a person who sees the expression of discomfort as selfish. Have they been dismissed in their own pain? Hard to believe, but many people are jealous of babies—the dynamic reveals their own frustration with not being allowed to express pain or be comforted.

Of course, you can see that it's possible that, in coming to the above conclusions, we inject our own personalities in exactly the same way!

Again, the old four Cs rule applies (context, clusters, congruence, and culture). We need to consistently pair our observations with a healthy level of open-mindedness and awareness of our own biases. If we don't stay mindful of all the possible ways we can heap distortion on top of distortion, then we quickly become lost in our own ungrounded assumptions and narratives.

Have you ever encountered an "armchair psychologist" who loved nothing more than to diagnose and psychoanalyze everyone they met? Such people can be annoying, but try hard not to be one of them, and be grateful that they are giving you such clear insight into *their* personality! Watch closely for the person who brands *everyone* around them a narcissist, claims to be an "empath," or pretends to have some special insight into other people.

The person who interprets everything in other people as a personal attack is strongly invested in an identity based on victimhood. The person who thinks that everyone is secretly in love with them (or else that everyone hates them) is telling you how they view themselves, and assuming everyone else's opinion accordingly. The person who is constantly judging others for not meeting their very high standards may be giving you a glimpse of the impossible standards they hold themselves to. People who generally think that others are kind-hearted, trustworthy, and valuable tend to possess those very traits themselves. And so on.

Naturally, our perceptions are influenced by our own personalities, but not exclusively determined by them. It is still possible that a person who is broadly happy with themselves can find someone else unpleasant or unlikeable. But even still, the way they describe that unlikableness will tend to show you something of their own personalities. For example, one person in a friend group is discovered to have committed a serious crime. While all his friends may be surprised and upset, they may each tell quite different stories about what that crime means, why it happened, and what they expect to happen next. For example, consider the mental models and filters that would have to be in place for a person to make each of the following observations:

- **Friend 1:** "He's just a bad person. Always was. I knew it from the beginning, so *I'm* not surprised in the least. Some people are just born evil."
- **Friend 2:** "Well, let him who is without sin cast the first stone, right? We've all done things we regret."

- **Friend 3:** "What a crazy world. You think you know someone. Just goes to show you can't trust people."
- **Friend 4:** "He didn't do it. End of story."
- **Friend 5:** "I don't know what happened. I just hope he's getting the help he needs. We're all so saddened by the whole thing" (note that here, this person is also making assumptions about other people's interpretations, imagining that they are all the same).

If you observed this wide range of reactions, not only would you be able to infer certain qualities about the people speaking, but you may also gather some useful information about the nature of the relationship each person shared with the man they were talking about:

- **Friend 1:** Quick to condemn, unable to forgive, black-and-white fixed mindset. This person also seems to want credit for seeing through the deception. Why might this be? They may value honesty but also take pride in their own shrewdness and intelligence and want people to understand that they are not able to be duped (even though they perhaps were).
- **Friend 2:** This person sees life in moral and possibly religious terms. They clearly value forgiveness, and base this on an

understanding of their own flaws. What in this person's own history might have made them value mercy, compassion, and forgiveness of sins?
- **Friend 3:** This person is viewing the situation in terms of trust. The criminal friend is seen to represent all humanity, and they are communicating that, in general, the world seems insane and unnavigable to them. The crime is a question of senselessness, not of right and wrong.
- **Friend 4**: What might this defensiveness mean? This may be a person so hurt by the prospect of the crime that they cannot even acknowledge it, or they are demonstrating just how much they value loyalty.
- **Friend 5:** This person has a default assumption of their friend's basic goodness and sees their deviation from this as temporary and unfortunate, requiring *help* rather than *punishment*.

Notice very carefully how people explain the good things and the bad things in life. Listen closely when you hear them guessing at other people's motivations or explaining to you the meaning of things in ambiguous or neutral situations. Combined with information you gather about their language, their non-verbal communication, and what they don't express, you can quickly build up incredibly rich models of other people—and with practice, you can get better at doing this without including your own distortions!

Identifying People's Values

Let's state explicitly a core tenet that we've been hinting at indirectly all throughout this book: **People's outsides reflect their insides**. In other words, their outwardly observable language, appearance, and behavior show us something of their hidden inner realities—if we know how to look.

People can wear masks and attempt to conceal how they really think and feel, but ultimately, a person cannot help but express who they are on the *inside* by what they do on the *outside*. The whole premise of becoming a better people-reader rests on the assumption that if we can accurately interpret and decode what we find on the outside, we can infer something about the inside.

Related to this is the idea that there is something lasting and stable inside people, and that this core of their being expresses itself in many different, fleeting ways. The sum of their consistent behavior, their choices, their interpretations, their language, their presentation and appearance, and everything they do, think, or say ultimately points back to this lasting and stable internal essence.

A big part of this core essence is a person's values—i.e., the principles they live by and the things they cherish most in life. If you understand what a person treasures in this way, then it's like having the key that will help you decode and understand all their behavior. You will understand what motivates them, what terrifies them, what captures their attention, and what will make them feel loved, validated, or threatened.

Knowing what people value is like understanding what fuel a vehicle runs on or what program has been installed on a computer. You can use this knowledge to communicate with them more effectively, to motivate and inspire them, to praise them, or even, if you wanted, to persuade or convince them of something. Knowing what they "run" on helps you understand why conflicts and misunderstandings occur and exactly how to resolve them.

Resource theory was first introduced by social psychologist Uriel G. Foa and colleagues in the seventies and serves as a framework for understanding social situations.

Of the theory, Foa et al. (1993) write, "At the heart of the theory is the insight that humans rarely satisfy their physical and psychological needs in isolation, and that social interactions and relationships provide the means by which individuals can obtain needed resources from others."

According to Foa, every human being has six primary "resource needs" stemming from childhood. We will all value these key resources in slightly different ways, however, prioritizing some over others according to our own unique histories and personal experiences.

Love

This is the resource of relationships, of social connection, warmth, trust, and belonging. It expresses the human need to be cared for and to care for others, to interact meaningfully with people one feels some kinship with, and to experience the intimacy/closeness that provides support and comfort. This need is also about family, sexual connection, social acceptance, and integration into a group.

Service

This resource is about the meaning that comes from being useful, instrumental, and valued by others for the work you do. It's all about integrity, duty, and fulfilled obligation. Service is about honor and pride, but also about the deep power of sacrifice and feelings of meaning and worth this confers on certain actions.

Status

The resource of status is not just about being recognized and acknowledged, but also about being appraised as broadly good and valuable, with a place in the world that is appreciated and cherished. Public respect, prestige, admiration, and deference are all a part of feeling as though one's contributions are valued, and in turn confer value on the one that has or offers them.

Goods

These are purely material possessions and belongings that supply a need for success, belonging, satisfaction, ease, or comfort. Goods of all types may have slightly different symbolic meanings for the people who own them, but they represent value that is tangible and observable.

Money

This is a material resource that is specifically financial. Monetary success is a resource that can also be translated into feelings of stability and comfort, or even luxury. To some it can represent opportunity, security, superiority, choice, or immunity from threat.

Information

The unknown is an eternal and sometimes threatening fact of life to contend with. We all have the human need for knowledge about what is happening in our world and why. If we understand a phenomenon, we can control and predict it. The resource of data often brings with it power, the ability to plan and pre-empt, not to mention the joy of an expanded view, of learning, clarity, and comprehension.

Each of us values and prioritizes one resource need above all others, and this resource drives our behavior.

Now, according to Foa, all six of these needs are held by all people everywhere—i.e., they are universal. You probably also noticed that they have significant overlap. For example, someone might have the need for the resource of money, but this is primarily because money allows them access to certain coveted goods . . . which may in turn be perceived as a way to win love and status.

There are also obviously very many more values than these six, but according to Foa, most of them can be reduced to one of these primary needs, or else is a combination of two or more of them. The need for faith and spiritual purpose, for example, can be seen as a blend of the resource of love and information, whereas someone's family orientation may be a blend of valuing service, status, and love. It's worth taking the time to consider your own values in this framework. There's a good chance that although you consider many things valuable, there's just one or two that you believe to be a clear priority.

So, how can you identify other people's values? Well, many of the methods already explored will yield plenty of information on what people care about and what they don't care about. A person who flatly fails the server test, for example, has clear and possibly unmet status and love needs, while people more likely to listen to the "relationship layer" instead of the "facts" later in the four ears model clearly favor love over information as a resource.

One surefire way to get an idea of someone's values is to listen closely to:

1. The things they complain about
2. The things they boast about
3. The things they worry about
4. Other behavioral and nonverbal cues

Pay attention to what people consistently gripe about as well as what they are proud and eager to share with you, and you will quickly realize what they consider most important. Listen also to how they interpret other people's behavior or explain things around them—which lens do they tend to default to when feeling sorry for or jealous of other people?

Money: Do they complain about bills or brag about how big their salary is? Do they pity people who earn modestly or consider big-earners enviable? This is the person who will describe their own motivations to you in terms of careers, mortgages, savings, investments, and so on.

Status: Do they get upset when their achievements are ignored or when they're embarrassed or called out? Do they totally relish praise, titles, awards, and honors? Are they very conscious of other people's status? This is the person who seeks praise but may also willingly court new responsibilities and positions of leadership.

Goods: Do they grumble about not having excellent quality things, or do they take immense pride in their homes, belongings or gadgets? Do they tend to talk about others in terms of what they own? This is the person who may have plenty of real-world knowledge about the value of objects, their maintenance, and how best to acquire them.

Service: Are they proud to tell you about the people they help, or do they often complain about being taken for granted or used? Are their personal heroes those who sacrifice, serve, help, and provide, and do they condemn selfish people? This is the person who dutifully remembers birthdays, takes time to honor etiquette and protocol, and takes family obligations very seriously.

Love: Do they boast about their popularity, likeability, or friendship groups? Does conflict and isolation upset them more than anything else? When someone is upset, do they automatically assume it's because they are feeling lonely or rejected? This may be the person who in social situations is primarily aware of other people's needs, addressing those as a priority over engaging with the factual content of the conversation. These people seek to connect first, ask questions later!

Information: Are they proud of what they know, or most upset by the idea of being ignorant or out of the loop? Do they judge the uneducated or the uncurious, but admire those they see as intelligent, shrewd, or correct? People who value information will often be networking, asking questions, fact-finding, verifying, teaching, learning, or, well . . . gossiping.

When people are feeling happy, content, and joyful, it's because their needs are met. So, when you see someone who seems to be totally comfortable and at peace, notice *why* they are. Is it because they're surrounded by friends and family (love) or because they are doing something they know will help others (service) or because they are safe and comfortable in their gorgeous home, surrounded by beautiful things they like (goods, money)?

Likewise, pay attention to all sorts of cues and hints about what makes people feel satisfied and content versus what puts them on edge. When you're talking to them, notice what they pay most attention to, what they engage with, and what they show their interest in. You might suddenly change the topic to your granddaughter and notice that it piques their interest, or you might notice that their entire demeanor changes once they start talking about money. Once you feel confident you've accurately identified people's main values, you may be surprised to see how everything—every word, gesture, and choice—ultimately stems from this deeper orientation.

Summary:

- The way people use language tells you a lot about who they are, what they value, and how they see the world. The "four ears" model says there are four layers to every message: the fact layer, the self-revelation layer, the relationship layer, and the appeal layer. As a neutral observer, you can learn a lot about social interactions or conflict by listening to *all* the other layers of meaning in a message, both spoken and heard.

- You can learn a lot about people by noticing all the ways their language is deliberately obscure or vague. The use of "weasel words" could imply deception, manipulation, uncertainty, avoidance, or deliberate obfuscation. Hedging language *may* also be used to soften, be polite, or be kind, but context matters. Notice *what* is being obscured or softened, notice deliberate wordiness and mystification, and notice what may be omitted from the message entirely.
- *One big question* allows us to watch the biases and assumptions that emerge in people as they observe and interpret other people. The big question is: "What do you think of this person?" and will reveal a lot about the speaker's character. Notice in particular how people explain other people's motivations and intentions.
- Noticing how people talk about themselves and others tells you a lot about what they value most. If you understand what a

person treasures, then you have the key to decode all their behavior. There are six universal resource needs: love, service, status, goods, money, and information. People tend to prioritize one, and this drives their behavior. To understand people's needs, listen closely to what they complain about, brag about, and worry about, as well as their various choices given the context.

Chapter 5: Digging Deeper to Learn What Really Makes People Tick

When we began this book, we started with people watching, where you stand apart from the social world, quite literally, and look on, making observations and inferences. Gradually, you learned more skills for learning to read people at closer range, listening to everything they were communicating with their bodies, their language, their voice, and what they *didn't* say.

We then went a little deeper and challenged our own biases and prejudices in order to have more genuine, more useful empathy for others. Beyond whether people are simply feeling this way or that way in the moment, what do they value on a more fundamental level? What emotional frame of reference do they tend to use, how do they see other people, how do they use language, and what kind of language do they respond to best?

In our closing chapter, we'll be looking at how our knowledge of a particular person will grow and deepen over time and how we can use our expanding understanding of them to accurately predict their future behavior. We'll also look at a few more "red flag" behaviors and warning signs and how you can start to really discern who is and isn't worth your trust.

The Three Levels of Knowing a Person

Personality psychologist and professor Dan McAdams believes that we move through three distinct stages of knowing other people, gradually getting closer and building a richer and more nuanced view of who they really are as people.

According to McAdams, the levels are:

Level 1—Self as social actor

Understanding general traits on a rather superficial level—and often exclusively in the present. For example, are they interested in the conversation or not? Do they seem more introverted or extroverted? Are they comfortable or do they appear mostly anxious? This was what we practiced when we engaged in a little people watching in the beginning of the book.

Level 2—Self as motivated agent

This is knowing a person in a little more depth and having knowledge about their motivations, their communication style, and their overall attitude and approach to life. By observing how people consistently behave over time, you can start to get an idea of the broader organizing patterns of their personality. What are their concerns, their coping mechanisms, their goals and strategies to achieving them? This was the level we explored when we considered the four ears model, people's values, and their answers to the "one big question."

Level 3—Self as Autobiographical Social Author

At level three, we start to synthesize information not just about what someone *does*, but who they really *are* at a core level. It takes time to work to this level because people are complex and contradictory and very often wear masks that deliberately conceal their true nature from others. At this level, we are no longer dealing with *types* but with completely unique flesh-and-blood individuals. This is the level we will be considering in our final chapter.

Crucially, this stage is about observing the way that people tell stories about themselves—i.e., the ways in which they are deliberate self-narrators—and that may include noticing the masks they choose to wear. According to McAdams, we are all constantly "selfing"—i.e., creating a coherent image of ourselves.

As you move from level one to two to three, you are making:

- More observations
- Over a longer period of time
- And including the person's deliberate attempts to be seen a certain way

As you observe, then, your perception both broadens and widens.

Let's say you observe some casual body language that tells you that someone is very interested in and concerned about the well-being of other people in social groups. On a level one reading, you might conclude that, at least at this moment in time, this person is behaving in ways that suggest that they are kind, are agreeable, and value relationships.

But let's say you *keep* observing this person. You notice that they often behave this way, but that they do it more in stressful or complicated situations, and especially in work contexts. You also notice that they don't behave this way with their very closest friends. This person gives plenty of other signs of being introverted, anxious, and *not* especially compassionate, by their own admission.

You realize that your own assumption about this person (a middle-aged woman and a mother) is that she is obviously caring and concerned about others, right? But as you keep observing, your interpretation of her kindness changes. You are at level two now and starting to notice that a big part of her ultra-caring and kind behavior is actually coming from her desire to manage and take control of social situations.

But your observation doesn't stop there. You soon realize that not only is she perfectly aware of the image she is portraying, but that she is portraying it deliberately. Why? Over many months and maybe years, you realize that this woman feels intensely uncomfortable and anxious in social situations, but she deals with this by going into hyper-caring mode, which allows her to effectively hide in a pre-existing social role and dissipate some of the tension she feels around big social groups. At her very core, this woman may even describe herself as anti-social.

Interestingly, your level three analysis actually contradicts your level one analysis! In other words, at level one you saw the mask, at level two you saw the purpose of the mask, and at level three you saw the real person behind the mask . . . and could start to guess at why they were wearing that mask.

The more you observe, the more data points you gather and the more you can start to see how these data points themselves interact. For example, most people are aware that they are being observed and that parts of them are available for others to see and interpret. While you are trying to read and interpret them, they are also simultaneously working to create and communicate some coherent sense of self, to construct a coherent image to show others, to conceal or emphasize certain things, or to protect others.

It's as though you are trying to read a story that is in the process of being written. In other words, the people we observe are always moving targets! Social dynamics are fluid and constantly changing, and your own point of reference is itself caught up in the process (because guess what, you are changing constantly too!).

Nevertheless, a good people-reader can and will read *anything*. If you notice that someone is deliberately putting on a particular mask in a social situation (that is, "acting" out a superficial role in a way discernible in level one), you might become curious about the structures at levels two and three that precipitated the choice to wear that mask.

The power of reading people across many levels is the realization that the person in front of you can be *both* compassionate and anti-social. Contradiction is not a problem but a part of who they are.

As you observe behavior consistently over time and across different contexts, you understand not just their superficial behavior in the moment, but also the beliefs and intentions behind that behavior. As you continue to observe, your observations and inferences become more nuanced and complex. You are gradually moving from observing what the person does to how they think and feel and, at the deepest level, to how they see themselves as people.

There are no surefire tips and tricks to learn to read people in this way; rather, your own powers of observation, empathy, and understanding will develop over time. People are not static images but more like novels or epic screenplays—it takes time for the story to unfold, and certain conclusions can only be made about the whole once you have gathered enough data and put it all into context.

Nevertheless, there are a few interesting questions you can use to start asking people to volunteer information from levels two and three. These questions are designed to query people's meaning-making capacities, their self-concept, their reflective awareness of who they are, and their unique values as expressed through what they focus on and how they interpret their world.

- **Ask them casually to share a story about their childhood.** For example, "What was the naughtiest thing you did as a kid?" This triggers the "self as autobiographical social author" mode and will invite people to share their constructed narratives. Listen closely to the genre of the story people tell, the role they play, the morale of that story. Someone might reply with mock surprise, insisting they were a good kid, while another may relish telling you just how much fun they had breaking the rules. The childhood story is not important—the picture they paint of their own story and personality *does* matter!
- **Use "why" questions.** For example, "So why do you think you picked accounting as a career?" You don't have to be intrusive about it, but framing questions this way

will prompt people to reveal their motivations, their goals, and the overall strategies they are using to cope with and navigate life. Again, the answer they supply is not important, but rather, the way they answer matters. Are they defensive, dismissive, proud, embarrassed . . . or confused that you think they "picked" their job in the first place?

- **Ask them about their own reading of a social situation.** For example, "Have you seen this news about [celebrity XYZ]? So crazy. Why do you think they did it?" You can frame this as idle chitchat or as asking for their advice or opinion. This is a variation on the "one big question" but takes it further, as you are asking the person to reveal how they make judgments of others and make sense of their actions. Once more, listen to the emotional reasoning and worldview behind the answer, and not the answer itself. Some people worship celebrities, others pity them . . . some worship them privately but "pity" them publicly!

Meltdowns, Tantrums, and Core Fears

Let's say you have an old friend you know inside out, but one day, they behave in a way so uncharacteristic of them, so unexpected, that you can't help thinking they've had an overnight personality transplant. Maybe they suddenly and dramatically lost their temper, maybe they had a strange anger outburst, or maybe they completely "lost it" with panic about something you never would have guessed was a problem.

Tantrums and meltdowns don't only happen to toddlers—adults experience them too, and when they do, they offer a brief glimpse into a world that is usually hidden. **Basically, we can understand a tantrum as resulting from a thwarted desire or core need.** This is interesting from a people-reading point of view because sometimes people's desires, expectations, demands, and requirements can be completely invisible—that is, until those expectations aren't met.

Call it a meltdown, a freakout, a rage, a tantrum, a sulk, a "strop," an outburst, or anything else—what you are witnessing is usually triggered by the person feeling overwhelmed by their own inability to cope with a situation. Thus, a child may throw a tantrum not because they desire a new toy from the supermarket but are denied; rather, the idea is that they throw the tantrum because they are unable to cope with the overwhelming sensations of their own disappointment and anger.

People may shut down, get overly emotional, lash out, yell, cry, hit things, or stomp their feet. These are all signals that a person's emotional resources are depleted. As an observer, you can learn a lot about people by considering the *way* they have tantrums and the things they tend to tantrum about.

Psychotherapist Dr. Homer B. Martin believes that there are actually two distinct tantrum profiles with their own thresholds, characteristics, and motivations, each shaped by early childhood experiences. Broadly, there is the **omnipotent personality** and the **impotent personality**.

Omnipotent personalities have a self-concept of strength, self-control, and competence. This is the person who expects much from themselves and who others may also have lofty expectations of.

Impotent personalities have a self-concept that is the opposite—they don't expect much of themselves and others likewise expect them to be helpless and passive. There may be little concern or care for others.

The interesting thing discovered by Dr. Martin is that omnipotent types seldom experience tantrums. They don't tend to protest when things don't go their way, and will find ways to accommodate others and make compromises.

When they *do* experience meltdowns, however, they may be filled with guilt for not meeting impossible demands, and their rage and upset tends to be self-directed, or else they withdraw.

Impotent personalities tend to tantrum more, and usually because they don't get their way (which, as you can imagine, might be perceived to happen often, because the impotent person is not perceived by themselves or others as capable of doing much). Their threshold for disappointment and despair is low, and when they have a meltdown, they tend to lash out at others, blaming them and treating other people or the world as the cause of their rage and upset. Naturally, this is a rather unhealthy way to cope and can often create more problems in the long run.

That's well and good, but how can we use the two profiles to help us read people more accurately? First of all, determine what type the person may be. If someone is having a meltdown, ask yourself:

- What provoked it? A large and near impossible task (suggests omnipotent) or a trivial one (suggests impotent)?

- Where is the focus of the anger and upset? On the self (omnipotent) or to others (impotent)?
- What is the desire for? Is this a reasonable demand (omnipotent) or an unreasonable one (impotent)?

By carefully noticing the size and nature of the demand, and the desire that has been thwarted, you can get a peek into how the person sees themselves:

Omnipotent types may have an internal locus of control (i.e., they feel they are in control of their own lives), may be responsible, active, mature, and have a growth mindset (i.e., "I don't know how to cope with this, but I can learn"). Their long-term response to such challenges is to find ways to do better next time. Their biggest fear may be that they do not reach extremely high standards and are *not good enough.*

Impotent types may have an external locus of control (i.e., they see their lives as controlled by outside forces), may be irresponsible, passive, and immature and have a fixed mindset (i.e., "I don't know how to cope with this, and I never will."). Their long-term response to such challenges is to feel victimized, avoid challenge, or get others to lower expectations. Their biggest fear is not that they don't reach a high upper limit, but fall below a lower limit—in other words that they are *bad*.

So, an impotent type may have a meltdown over a minor task or demand that they have little reason to believe they can't accomplish, for example, meeting a tight but doable work deadline. They may deal with the stress of the situation by lashing out at their boss or colleagues, sulking, or framing the situation as one in which they are being targeted. Their tantrum will be an attempt to have their boss extend the deadline, which is something they may feel entitled to. An omnipotent type, on the other hand, may be just as stressed and unhappy about the deadline, but have a meltdown that consists solely of them withdrawing and getting mad at *themselves*.

If you observe a person having a tantrum, consider everything else you know about them. What is their overall self-concept? What are their expectations of themselves and others? What are the expectations that other people have of them? Is victimhood and passivity a part of this person's identity, or are they perfectionists? What does the outburst tell you about their values, their expectations, and how they see their own level of competence?

Discovering People's Core Fears

Psychotherapist Karen Horney's "basic anxiety" model suggests that all people have a core fear that influences and shapes their entire personality, mostly through the person's attempts to defend and protect against that perceived fear.

Tantrums and meltdowns can point to people's core fears, and these core fears can provide enormous insights into the way people think, feel, and behave. Knowing what a person fears helps you predict how they will behave, and helps you make sense of their communication style, their goals, and their way of coping with challenge and conflict.

Broadly, there are five "universal themes of loss" that people can gravitate toward. Naturally, we all fear these things, but each of us tends to have one in particular that, due to our childhood conditioning, is perceived as most threatening:

1. **Abandonment**, which is the fear of losing love, being rejected, or else being left behind.
2. **Loss of identity**, which is the fear of losing the self or else the knowledge of the self.
3. **Loss of meaning**, which is the fear of losing sense, understanding, or coherence.

4. **Loss of purpose**, which is the fear of losing the ability or opportunity to contribute value.
5. **Loss of life**, which is the fear of death, but also of illness, pain, and suffering.

When observing tantrums or meltdowns, you may notice that the perceived loss is often one of identity or purpose—i.e., losing the ability to cope with life's challenges, or else losing the dignity and pride that comes with that coping. People can also lash out due to fear of perceived abandonment or rejection or plain old stress, however—which is a form of loss of life.

To identify someone else's core fear:

Step 1: Notice what someone frames as a problem or concern. What is capturing their attention as a problem, what are they complaining about, or who or what do they label as a threat?

Step 2: Get curious and ask questions about the problem identified in step 1. Some good questions include:

- Why exactly is this thing bothering you?
- What do you think will happen next?
- What's so bad about that?
- What are you worried you will lose?

Step 3: Listen closely to their answer and try to empathetically hear the emotional content behind it. You may need to ask a few questions in succession, as people are often not even themselves sure what they're afraid of and will point to many other things before identifying the core fear.

Sometimes you can conduct the above three steps in a straightforward way; other times you may need to merely watch for signs and clues (for example, when a tantrum is underway!). One thing you can watch out for is what seems to reduce any observed anxiety. If a person instantly becomes soothed when people appear to comfort them, their core fear may be abandonment. Similarly, a person who instantly calms down when a scary situation is clearly explained, or when they are reassured of the value of their contribution, may be demonstrating core fears of loss of meaning and purpose, respectively.

What People's Friendships Say about Them

One fascinating outward manifestation of people's inner worlds is actually people—namely, the people they deliberately choose to keep around them. We already know that if someone chooses to dress in a particular way, if they engage in certain behaviors or consistently express themselves in certain ways, it tells us something about who they are. Well, the same can be said for the kinds of people they surround themselves with. "You are the company you keep" is not just an old saying but may be quite literally true.

A person's social network is not just a crystallized outward reflection of the way they see themselves, how they interact with others, and what they value, but all these things *over time*. Your social network is also quite difficult to fake, so in terms of a social signal you can learn to read, it's pretty foolproof.

A recent study shows that you can actually predict a lot about a person by observing the friendships they keep (Laakasuo et al. 2016). Researchers at the University of Helsinki investigated more than twelve thousand British people and compared their personality traits with their friendship style. Here's what this, and other research studies, have found:

If Someone Has a Small Friendship Group

This may indicate intelligence (Li and Kanazawa 2016). The authors found that on the whole social people tended to be happier people—with one exception, namely that highly intelligent people tend *not* to derive satisfaction from more social engagement. They may prefer spending energy on intellectual pursuits or non-social projects and derive more satisfaction and meaning from these.

But interpret with care. A person with a very small social group *who appears to be happy that way* may be more intelligent than average, whereas someone with a small social group who is distressed by the fact may be of average intelligence. They may have few friends but not by choice.

If Someone's Friends Are all Long Distance

This may indicate a greater openness to experience (which is one of the Big Five personality traits), especially if the friendship group is very diverse and includes people from all walks of life. But here again, caution is advised when making interpretations.

Person A may have the bulk of their friend group living hundreds of miles away, but only because these are old friends from their hometown. They may have no friends in their current city despite living there for years. While their long-distance friendships may suggest loyalty and consistency, they do not necessarily suggest openness—apart from, perhaps, the openness to travel more for one's friends.

Person B, on the other hand, may have a wide group of diverse friends from all over the world because they are curious and accepting of everyone and have a wide range of interests that connect them to people of all kinds. Long-distance friendships can also suggest that the person has traveled extensively and that they value genuine connection in their friends and not just convenience and proximity.

If Someone Is "Popular"

This may indicate an awareness and appreciation of social hierarchies. This is a person who has one way or another succeeded in being likeable, well-known, and socially involved. This could suggest high social intelligence, a high value placed on status and information, and a strong need for group affiliation and belonging.

Many of us have high school to blame for associating popularity with cruelty and manipulative personality traits, but actually popular people tend to be high in agreeableness (i.e., they're nice) and tend to work hard to harmonize with others, communicate well, and reduce conflict. Of course, when it comes to people-reading, the nature of the attention a person receives from their friendship group matters. Being well loved by your local community is one thing; being a minor social media celebrity who is never far from the next scandal is quite another.

If Their Friendships Are very Long-Lasting

This points to overall agreeable and easy-going personalities. Think about it: A person who is overly exacting, dramatic, intolerant, and unreliable will seldom keep friends in the long term. That's usually reserved for people who are more relaxed and accommodating.

Notice also whether someone has maintained friendships from childhood or school—it could point to valuing tradition over novelty and suggest the person is loyal and trustworthy. Someone who doesn't seem to have anyone in their world that they've known longer than a few months is telling you that somehow, they endure frequent social disruptions. This may or may not be their fault—you'll need to gather more data to find out.

If Their Friends Are all Solid, Dependable, and the Same Gender

This suggests the person is conscientious—i.e., they take their responsibilities seriously, are organized, hard-working, and generally goal-directed. Conscientious people tend to select other conscientious people as friends. Pay attention when a social circle contains people who have respectable and enduring careers, and who are law-abiding, trustworthy, and thoughtful.

Likewise, a red flag is if someone has a social circle consisting exclusively of people who are unreliable, tend to break rules, or are perceived or perceive themselves as outsiders and misfits. A mixed group of friends could point to someone who values diversity and variety and may hold more cosmopolitan opinions.

If Someone Spends an Enormous Amount of Time Socializing

Regardless of the number of friends people have, pay attention to how much of their time overall is devoted to being with others. They could highly value relationships and other people and have a strong need for affiliation and connection with others. On the other hand, the quality of the interaction matters too. You may observe someone who is seemingly always with others but the relationships are shallow, and you might wonder whether the person has a fear of being alone.

Naturally, having a big and busy friend group could be more appropriate at certain stages of life than others. People in their early twenties may derive a huge amount of their identity from their friends, hobbies, and interests, while a mid-thirties person may have no friends to speak of besides their spouse, children, and close relatives.

If Someone's Friendship Group Contains Plenty of Exes

There are many ways to read this (no surprises there!) so pay attention to other clues and signs. A person who has several ex-partners in their friendship group may signal that they are extremely agreeable and capable of salvaging healthy friendships even after romantic relationships end. Such people may be demonstrating a genius for resolving conflict and for careful boundary management (given that the friendships are happy, of course). The big clue will be in how people talk about their exes—this will tell you what they value, how they resolve conflict, and the importance they give to friendship in relation to romantic relationships.

On the other hand, beware of people whose friendship group contains many *would-be* romantic partners. If a person is actively maintaining countless unrequited loves in their orbit, this could suggest poor or unclear boundaries, status games, and the need for a perpetual ego boost! For the same reason, be on the alert for people whose "friends" only include fans, colleagues, clients, or people incentivized in some way to show interest.

If Someone's Friends Are all Strangers to One Another

Finally, notice whether someone is part of a friendship group or whether the people they know and care about are all in effect isolated from one another. A person who has a miscellaneous mix of curated people who are not friends with each other may be demonstrating a more deliberate, intentional, and strategic approach to friendships, valuing those who fit a detailed set of criteria. This is the person who is picky about friends and goes out deliberately to seek them.

The person who is happy to make friends with an entire group, conversely, shows that they are less fussy and particular about getting on perfectly with others. They may be more accepting and go-with-the-flow types.

Those who prefer to socialize one-on-one tend to enjoy going into depth with others, talking intently, and knowing each other on a deep level, while those who prefer to socialize in larger groups tend to enjoy the overall vibe of a group, and do not necessarily crave deep-and-meaningful conversations. They may find it more important that a friend is broadly loyal and good company than that they are kindred spirits who agree with them on everything. In the same way, people who prefer big-group socializing may make friends quickly and easily but take a long time to trust on a deep level, while those who prefer one-on-one time may take a long time to trust, but when they do, they trust completely and permanently.

Predicting Social Behavior

One of the key aims in science is not just to understand natural phenomena, but to be able to predict how those phenomena will evolve in the future. The "science" of people-reading is just the same. They say that the best predictor of future behavior is past behavior, so it stands to reason that having deep insight into how people behave in the present can help us master the superpower of predicting how they'll behave in the future.

In the social world, knowing how to do this is not just an academic exercise, of course, but something that allows us to effectively identify people we can and cannot trust, to anticipate and prepare for behavior, and to pre-emptively tailor our communication so that it always has the best possible outcome.

Unfortunately, a big part of sizing people up in social situations is about learning to spot red flags, avoid difficult personalities, and steer clear of dynamics you know have no chance of evolving in your favor. You need to know who to trust.

According to Robin Dreeke, an ex-behavior analyst who worked with the FBI for twenty years, the key thing to remember is that **almost all people can be expected to do one thing: act in their own best interests**. This isn't as cynical as it sounds; after all, people can and do act altruistically *in addition to* caring about their own interests, but we would be foolish to imagine that this is not a constant consideration for most of us, most of the time.

If you've been absorbing and applying the many approaches and methods described in this book so far, you've probably already come a long way in identifying those people who are most likely to deserve your trust . . . and those who might not be. Luckily, Dreeke offers some advice for identifying exactly what people actually think is in their best interests, and therefore predicting how they will act in the future.

Five Clues to Future Behavior

When you're observing people and trying to interpret and understand their behavior, try asking the following questions to help you zero in on their motivation. This can be considered an advanced form of perspective-taking.

Do they think that they could possibly benefit from your success?

People tend to more likely help those whose success they believe will reflect well on them. People will directly or indirectly associate themselves with their projects, help them, defend them, and promote them, because they have a vested interest in that success for their own reasons.

How can you use the answers you get to this question?

First, you could ask questions to help you understand people's goals and objectives (level two stuff!) and determine for yourself how well your goals align with theirs. If they do, proactively share this fact and you will win them to your side. If they don't, avoid trying to persuade them—you already know they will never be quite as invested.

You could also use this question to help you understand why someone may be showing a sudden interest in helping you or someone else. Whether this benefits you or not, be crystal clear about what's in it for *them*.

Do they anticipate having a long relationship with you?

If you think there's a chance you may have to associate with someone for a long time to come, you're going to be more motivated to work on cultivating a good relationship.

To apply this, simply remember that the more time, the more trust. You can predict, for example, that temporary employees are more likely to cut corners than permanent ones who have more to lose if the working relationship sours.

Likewise, put people's opinions and what they say into context. This is one of the reasons people are sometimes encouraged to date within their social networks rather than seek out perfect strangers on dating apps—people are far more likely to be honest, behave well, and keep their promises when they know it's possible they will encounter the person again someday.

One clever trick to assess their expectations of a future relationship is to ask them to participate in a long-term goal with you. If their attention or enthusiasm drops, it's a good sign they are not planning to stick around. Likewise notice if they regularly use "I" and seldom "we."

Good signs include being able to adjust themselves to you, willingness to share a secret with you, and willingness to call in favors on your behalf (because they have a hope that, in the long term, you might be able to repay them).

Can they actually do what they promise?

Reliability basically means that someone's behavior is highly predictable. If they say they will be there at noon, your prediction that they will be there at noon is likely to be correct. In other words, you can trust them. But reliability is not the only predictor of future behavior—the person also has to be competent to actually do what they say they will.

You can't predict how someone will act if they don't show signs of reliability, a quality that's composed of competence and diligence. Just because someone wants to do something for you, it doesn't mean they're competent to do so. And even if they are, it doesn't mean they're diligent enough to get the job done or to carry it out. Too many people can get confused in reading others because they pay attention to the sincerity of the promises made—but a person can genuinely *want* to do something, and they may even believe they will, without having the discipline or ability to actually follow through.

To put this into practice, ignore what people say and watch what they do. It's not unusual, for example, for ambitious Type A people to believe and claim that they can achieve more than they really can. You'd be a fool for taking their word for it without doing your own due diligence. Do they have a track record for overpromising and under-delivering?

Remember that reliability and predictability are about probabilities *over time*—you cannot determine someone's reliability after observing just one behavior. Look for patterns and the behaviors that are most consistent.

Notice if there is any consistent difference between actions and words. Look for signs of trustworthiness and diligence. These include communicating openly, simply, and plainly. Look for transparency and a person who takes things seriously. Secrecy, complexity, and mismatch between words and actions are always warning signs.

To assess overall reliability, observe if someone communicates verifiable specifics, if they take responsibility for their actions, and if they are transparent about their shortcomings. A reliable person will *want* to demonstrate their accountability, while an unreliable one will shy away from requests for commitment.

Do they know how to communicate?

Perhaps the biggest clue to a person's character is their use of language, in particular the way they speak about other people. If they consistently speak of others in a negative way, if they consistently resort to blame, and if they consistently use manipulation and judgment, then you know you are dealing with someone with their own issues.

Watch out for exaggeration and boasting, the constant need for "debate," evasiveness, or any other communication style that is marked by negativity. And yes, this does include sarcastic humor and playful self-deprecation!

Notice how a person communicates, and you gain insight into how they think. This tells you what you can expect from this person in general—how they will resolve conflict, how they are likely to frame challenges, and where their focus will always tend to gravitate to. In other words, you may just be getting a preview about how this person could talk about *you*.

To assess someone's communication style, observe if they actively seek your opinions, address your priorities in conversation, validate your perspectives, and offer you choices, indicating a respectful and inclusive approach to interaction.

Are they basically stable?

By stability, Dreeke means emotional maturity, self-awareness, and the kind of common sense that belongs to people you can genuinely rely on to keep it together. It's important not to get too distracted by the *reasons* for someone's instability. Sure, a person may have experienced genuine trauma, loss, and stress in the past that is influencing them now. They may have had to contend with poor mental or physical health, abuse, or insecurity, and of course we can and should have compassion.

Nevertheless, our compassion should not cloud our accurate appraisal of a person and our reasonable prediction of their future behavior.

To read someone's level of emotional stability and maturity, watch closely how they respond to change and challenge. Stable people will be difficult to budge. They don't scare easily. They tend toward rational, considered decisions and cannot be manipulated easily. They tend to be content with things.

To spot low stability, simply look for signs of chaos, drama, and high volatility in everyday life. Everyone's life goes through change and transition now and again, but look for patterns of consistent instability, such as frequent breakups, ongoing fights with friends, recurrent job loss, repeated minor run-ins with the law, careless and disordered behavior, rapidly cycling extremes, a consistent lack of any routine or structure, and "mixed messages."

Summary:

- There are three levels of knowing a person: At level one we witness only their behavior and the mask they wear, at level two we see more of their goals and coping mechanisms, and at level three we start seeing the way they choose to self-narrate. Learning to know a person on a very deep level takes time, patience, and the willingness to embrace subtlety, even contradiction. Ask them *why* questions or for their interpretations on things, especially their childhoods.
- Meltdowns and tantrums are revealing. Tantrums result from a thwarted desire or core need and are triggered by the person feeling overwhelmed by their own inability to cope with a situation. Observe whether a person is an omnipotent (self-concept of strength) or impotent (self-concept of weakness) type—this will give a clue about

their core fear. Observe the tantrum trigger, the focus, and the thwarted desire.
- There are five core fears, which are broadly about loss of love, of identity, of meaning, of purpose, or of life. Knowing what a person fears helps you predict their behavior, their communication style, their goals, and their coping strategies.
- "You are the company you keep" is true, and people's friendship groups tell you a lot about them. Notice how many friends they have, how far away they live, how often they see them, and what kind of people they socialize with.
- Remember that almost all people can be expected to do one thing: act in their own best interests. To predict a person's trustworthiness toward you, ask about whether they stand to benefit from your success, whether they anticipate a long relationship with you, their communication skills, their overall stability, and their actual ability to do what they promise they will.

www.ingramcontent.com/pod-product-compliance
Lightning Source LLC
Chambersburg PA
CBHW060606080526
44585CB00013B/698